O9-BTO-858

Law in Film

Law in Film

Resonance and Representation

David A. Black

University of Illinois Press

Urbana and Chicago

© 1999 by the Board of Trustees of the University of Illinois
Manufactured in the United States of America
1 2 3 4 5 C P 5 4 3 2 1

∞ This book is printed on acid-free paper.

Library of Congress Cataloging-in-Publication Data
Black, David A. (David Alan), 1959–
Law in film : resonance and representation / David A. Black.
p.   cm.
Includes bibliographical references and index.
Filmography: p.
ISBN 0-252-02459-1 (cloth : acid-free paper)
ISBN 0-252-06765-7 (pbk. : acid-free paper)
1. Justice, Administration of, in motion pictures. I. Title.
PN1995.9.J8B63   1999
791.43'655—ddc21   98-25506
CIP

For my family

Contents

Acknowledgments   ix

Introduction   1

Part 1

Fundaments of Legal and Cinematic Narrative

1. Toward a Working Definition of Narrative   13

2. Law and Film as Narrative Regimes   34

Part 2

Knowing Law in Film

3. Genre and Its Alternatives   55

4. History, Genre, and Reflexivity   87

Part 3

Regimes of Writing

5. Metaphorical Bridges   99

6. Legal Scholarship Looks at Film   109

7. The Forensics of Film Reception   141

Part 4

Power, Prison, Pain

8. Bound and Determined   161

Filmography   185

Index   189

Acknowledgments

This book has benefited from support, input, and critique of a number of kinds from a number of sources. One source is my doctoral dissertation, "Narrative Film and the Synoptic Tendency" (New York University, 1989), several chapters of which I draw on here. My dissertation advisor, Robert Stam, and the members of my core committee, Edward Branigan and William Simon, provided criticism and reaction of a materially helpful nature throughout the life cycle of that project. My supplemental readers, Robert Sklar and Antonia Lant, offered insightful readings and suggestions for development.

Seton Hall University has provided support of more than one kind. Some of the research for this book was supported by a summer stipend from the University Research Council. In addition, my colleagues in the Department of Communication have offered insight and interest throughout the several phases of this project, from proposal to appearance in print. In particular, Donald McKenna and Christopher Sharrett have been mainstays of encouragement and practical assistance. I am very grateful to both of them for their help.

Through the sharing of his extraordinary film collection, the late William Everson enriched—and still enriches—the studies and scholarship of every person associated with the Department of Cinema Studies at New York University. In my case, additionally, he was generous and forthcoming with advice about courtroom films; it is through him that I learned of, and was able to watch, *The Man Who Wouldn't Talk*, an interesting and obscure film which otherwise would not figure in this book.

In 1989 and again in 1991, I conducted a graduate seminar at New York University on the subject of "The Representation of Legal Processes in Fiction Film." Discussions with students in those classes played a significant role in my perspective on the topic during a formative stage in that perspective. In particular, I have benefited over the years from ongoing explorations of topics in this area in conversations with Cynthia Lucia, whose work on the female lawyer film of the 1980s (currently in dissertation form) represents a major contribution to law-film studies.

At the University of Illinois Press, Ann Lowry took an early interest in this project and saw it through in a thoroughly collegial, professional, and supportive manner. I am grateful for her guidance at various potentially difficult forks in the road. Taking up the manuscript in the latter stages of production, Theresa Sears facilitated its passage through final revisions and corrections, to the immense benefit of the text. August Gering's copyediting raised not only the quality of the prose but also the level of our national reserves of ink: the unnecessary comma never had a worthier foe.

Over the years, many friends, colleagues, and family members have contributed, in one way or another, to the growth of this book. Some have engaged in conversation; some have pointed me toward interesting and relevant films; some have shared their expertise in legal scholarship during my "visit" to that domain. Among those whom I wish to thank for their help and enthusiasm are David Bénéteau, Barbara Aronstein Black, Martha Hollander, Richard Kass, Jacob Levich, Judy Lieb, Michael Macrone, Ivone Margulies, Brigitte Peucker, Suzanne Samuels, and Tom von Gunden.

Finally, I offer thanks to six friends who—individually, cumulatively, and sometimes collectively—have done so much to set the tone of intellectual environment in which this project has grown (and much of the rest of life) that I cannot begin to sort the threads, nor imagine what I and my work would consist of without their influence. Special thanks, then, to Edward Branigan, Christine Laennec, Roberta Pearson, Dan Plonsey, Jennifer Rycenga, and Michael Syrotinski.

Law in Film

Introduction

A Place on the Shelf

On offer in this book is a tour—negotiated in advance, and guided, by a narrative theorist—of a succession of stretches of confluence between and among the cultural, textual, and historical channels of film and law.

Film and law are two of our most prolific and important narrative regimes. While there is more to their interaction than what is on the screen, a useful starting point is the observation that film *indefatigably* represents law. Thus, as a phenomenon of potential interest to a narrative theorist, film about law is doubly determined, precisely because it is, at one and the same time, both film (one narrative regime) and about law (another).

My interest in the phenomenon of law in film encompasses what may be called the roots and branches of this double determination. The roots include a number of cultural, formal, and ideological points of contact and shared history between the world of law and the world of film—including, not exclusively but very importantly, their mutual commitment to narrative as a central organizing principle. The branches include metaphorical cross-borrowings, relevant developments in legal pedagogy (where film has started to play a role), and existing scholarship of various kinds. Something is at stake for each of a number of parties, including audiences, theorists, and educators. This results in a kind of "vertical" orientation, a cross-section of cultural, cognitive, ideological, pedagogical, and theoretical concerns.

Film represents law, and this book will explore, on several fronts, the phenomenon of the representation of law in fiction film. Indeed, this book is about the very fact that there is such representation; about what it means for there to be such representation; about what theorists and teachers have done as a consequence of there being such representation. In sum, this book is about *the fact of the representation of one important cultural practice in the signifying terms of another.*

If the intertwinings of film and law at the levels of theory and cultural history are the roots and branches of this project, then actual films about law—*The Wrong Man, Witness for the Prosecution, A Question of Silence*—might best be described as the leaves. Filmic texts have a somewhat unusual role to play in this book, and both my and the reader's interests will be best served by my spelling out that role here. Specifically, and chiefly, this book is *not* a survey of films about law, nor of any significant subset of them. The films I discuss are chosen exclusively for their value as examples, relevant for various reasons at various points in the book, of how to talk about what I am talking about in the way that I am suggesting it be talked about. Relatively few films are treated in real depth, certainly far fewer than would be if this were a book of essays about individual films. Films about law end up not necessarily playing any greater a role, as antecedent or illustrative texts, than written sources do; an article by a law professor about the use of film in the classroom is as likely a candidate for analysis in this book as is a film about a trial.

In short, *Law in Film*'s place on the shelf is not among the video guides, nor even among the genre surveys, but among works concerned with narrative theory in engagement with the historical and operational premises of specific representational regimes.

Origins and Scope of the Project

The thing that first interested me about this area of inquiry was the courtroom film. In particular, I was intrigued by what I saw, and still see, as a kind of narrative overdetermination. The (real) courtroom was *already* an arena or theater of narrative construction and consumption, and so was the movie theater. The representation of court proceedings in film, therefore, brought about a doubling up, or thickening, of narrative space and functionality—a bit like playing two baseball games on the same diamond at the same time.

It was quickly apparent to me that the process of gaining theoretical purchase on this phenomenon would involve "stepping back" from close textual analysis of courtroom scenes and looking at (and for) the underlying connections. What I did not quite bargain for was the fact that, for each step back, one does not find that a single new topic enters into view but rather that exponentially more topics do. To begin with, *courtroom film*, as a token of choice and organization, became *films about law*—which, depending on one's definition of *about*, opens the category up at least to detective films and prison films and possibly to virtually every commercial fiction film ever made. (For better or worse, I tend to take a rather inclusive view of *about*.)

Furthermore, the historical and ideological matters lying outside of the films themselves, but providing the common ground that makes for the overdetermined quality of those films, are rather vast: they include such things as the cultural centrality of narrative (i.e., logically and historically prior to the centrality of narrative to particular cultural institutions such as film and law); the currency of metaphors such as "witness" and "camera," in general and as they have identifiably surfaced in law and film's theoretical dealings with each other; pedagogical concerns relating to the relationship between theory and professionalism, as indexed, in particular, by the use of films about law by legal instructors; and so forth.

I do not apologize for the sprawl. In fact, it is what has kept me intrigued and interested in this area for a long time. Nonetheless, in this book I have tried to reckon with it and to package all of these matters in such a way that, at the very least, each major section has a clear center of gravity (textual analysis, institutional history, theoretical position statement, etc.). Ultimately, though—and, come to think of it, initially—they all link up. This is not an abstract assertion of an underlying unity for which I yearn but a straightforward report of my experience with the topic. Looking at a courtroom film might trigger consideration of some aspect of legal procedure, which might lead to writings by legal scholars, who might turn out to have used films in their classrooms, which raises comparative questions about the status of legal pedagogy and film theory . . .

I recognized this heterogeneity of source materials and their interrelationships in the next-to-earliest days of my involvement with the topic and responded to it by permanently abandoning the strategy of organizing my work as a series of textual studies of individual films. Such a strategy, in my view, would seriously disserve the complexity and vibrancy of the topic. To some extent this is circular reasoning: the turning point was the realization that "the topic" was precisely this heterogeneity and not, for example, "the formal evolution of the court-room film." In fact, I see no problem with this (mine is hardly the first book ever not to be organized as a series of textual exegeses). But it needs stating, for two reasons. First, the matter of defining what "films about law" are remains a central concern, even (and, I would argue, especially) in the course of reckoning in the large with matters of law-film interaction at a variety of levels. Second, readers' expectations tend to run in the direction of a genre-ish orientation based on film-by-film analysis. I know this because, in talking casually or otherwise about the project, I have fielded many questions over time that reveal it. Our culture has provided law and film, in their union, numerous and diverse plots of land in which to grow and intermingle. But the notion of a book about law in film still powerfully evokes the image of a critical walk along the linear path of textual analysis. I have no quarrel with the basic idea of writing a book about one detective or courtroom film after another, and I would take great interest in any book that approached these genres in a really probing way; but for better or worse, my own attention remains drawn in the large to the syncretic field of entanglements between law and film as narrative, representational, critical, and pedagogical regimes, and to the project of mapping out a path through that field.

My purposes in this mapping are navigational rather than oceano-graphic; that is, I wish to show a particular way through an expanse rather than catalog it. Heterogeneous as my approach may be, it is still selective. After all, at its *most* inclusive, a phrase like "film and law" includes a lot more than I will include here.[1] What I propose to map out is not the entirety of what might be referred to by that phrase but those historical, theoretical, and interpretive issues that—while still large—are relatively closely derived from a consideration of the overdeter-mined nature of the representation of law in film.

Some of the problems I have had to grapple with in the course of navi-gating this subject matter are theoretical problems relating to such matters as genre, reflexivity, criteria of text-corpus membership, recon-ciling theory and other "levels" of analysis with each other, and the relationship between the theory and the topic itself. While I intend to steer clear of a lavishly "confessional" style of exposition, I nonethe-less choose not to be entirely poker-faced about the fact of this grap-pling. The project has always been, and is now, an interpretive one.

What Law? What Film?

In spite of my fascination with parallels, there are differences between the criteria of inclusion I am applying to law and those I am applying to film.

The "film" part of "law and film," here, is made up of all fiction films in which legal processes are depicted. "Legal processes," in this film-filtering sense, include investigation and detection, trial, and punishment. My treatment of these phases of legal process as they appear in film will not be symmetrical or even-handed, as measured either by pages devoted or by theoretical weight; however, I will try to be clear as to where the focus lies at any given point.

This algorithm of inclusion, of course, casts an enormous cinematic net; in fact, so stated, it includes just about every imaginable fiction film. This is and is not an issue. To the extent that it is an issue, it will be addressed in the section "Genre and Its Alternatives," which will deal with the whole question of the specification of a corpus of films (which is a different matter here than in a genre study but is important enough to bring up). On the other hand, the vast sweep of the law-in-film criterion is *not* an issue, in the sense that I do not aim to draw a circle around anything or to set limits. I aim, rather, to start something; at least, from the point of view of my grasp of it, I am starting something. In a sense, the things I am proposing only have to be right in a significant number of cases, even if they are wrong in others; if someone else comes along and points out legal and/or filmic systems for which what I am saying does not hold up, that's fine. On the other hand, if by keeping it a bit abstract I make it possible for other people (or even myself, at some future point) to revisit these ideas and find new interest or applicability in them, that's fine too.

My approach to defining "law," as it pertains to this study, is somewhat less binary and more heuristic. Pressed for a first approximation, I would probably say that the center of gravity is Anglo-American criminal justice; and, as measured on the overall scale of possible types and histories of law, such a characterization would probably stand. But it would be misleading to present this as a rigorous criterion of study or inclusion. The heuristic or explorative approach leads to a consideration of distinctly other things and other perspectives: the existence of different legal systems; disagreement and debate among legal scholars as to the suitability of narrative theory as a way of understanding law (any law); friction between vocational training and theoretical undermining in the pedagogical sphere; and so forth.

Moreover, given my cross-sectional strategy with respect to strata of theory, practice, and pedagogy, any attempt to define law by strict geopolitical or jurisdictional criteria will run aground on such things as an evening spent at New York University Law School viewing and discussing *A Question of Silence*—a Dutch film that depicts Dutch legal processes but has received a lot of international attention for its treatment of matters of narrativity and the relativity of legal truth (and receives a lot of attention from me toward the end of this book). I would not wish to have to say whether, during such an evening, we were dealing chiefly with film theory, Anglo-American legal pedagogy, Dutch law, or gender politics (both in the film and among the discussants). It was all of these; and in large part it is the historical fact of such syntheses and convergences that interests me.

Coming at it the other way, the "law" I am reckoning with could be described, again as a first approximation, as law that shares fiction film's grounding in narrativity. This tautology is not as useless as it may sound—after all, the entire project springs from the fact that these issues circulate in both law and film, and even such a self-fulfilling definition would leave one with plenty to do and plenty to say. In some respects, the tautological account comes closer to the spirit of the project than a predicate like "Anglo-American law." At the very least, such a predicate must bow before real reflection and investigation.

In essence, this work remains a theoretical essay: an attempt to take a small number of generative insights, go forward with them, and renegotiate the field of inquiry—if only to see what it will look like.

Why This Book Is Not about Television

Film theorists have perhaps clung too tightly to the habit of talking about "film" as if it were an isolated unit of practice and meaning—as if, moreover, hours clocked in the movie theater actually accounted for the acquisition of visual literacy and competence in the cognition of kinetic narrative. For some time it has been the case that such competence comes first from television, not from "film" (at least not film in the traditional, dream-in-the-dark, cinephiliac sense experienced and speculated about by film theorists in the first three quarters of this century).

At the best of times, then, theories of film—how we learn to understand film; questions of the relation between film and language; the various economies of attention and cognition involved in watching film; analogies between film and dream or film and hypnosis—are probably being allowed too idealistic an existence or giving too much credit for filmic literacy to film. This is not to say that television has not had a share of the attention; but the underlying model is still one of film theory, extensible to television.

In the case of the representation of law, the matter is made more complex by the fact that television (even American commercial television alone) adds hundreds of thousands of hours of screen time to the filmic body under consideration. These hours, moreover, take a number of different forms: fictional programs (about police, private detectives, lawyers, judges, prison officials); documentary or news coverage (especially "Court TV"); and even hybrids between game shows and some kind of reality programming ("Superior Court," "Divorce Court"). The representation of law on television, in short, grows or shrinks to fit just about any programming form, scripting idea, or visual subidiom at which it can be thrown.

Yet this book is not about "Court TV." It is not even about "Perry Mason." The representation of law on television is not unapproachable, but it is not, in my view, suited to the achievement of the initial goals of the process of staging this particular meeting between legal and filmic history and practice. I am convinced that a more cogent set of observations will come from a relatively—though, I must add, not very—restricted scope. Much of what I will say here, I believe, might suggest ways of understanding the representation of law on television; or, that representation might serve as a source of test cases and occasions for troubleshooting what I present. But to center the project from the outset around television would be to leapfrog over what I believe to be important points more readily retrievable from a focus on film.

The Structure of the Book

There are four major parts to this book, each of which contains one or more chapters. Each of the four parts stakes out a particular way of negotiating the law-film relationship.

Part 1: Fundaments of Legal and Cinematic Narrative   Included here, by way of prolegomenon to the comparative theoretical work that follows, is an attempt to develop a working definition of narrative (chapter 1), not specifically bound to the study of either law or film, but relevant to both. Chapter 2 looks at the two chief objects of study in parallel; that is, at this stage, our concern is not (yet) with the appearance of law in films but rather with identifying and expanding on a number of similarities and convergences between law and film themselves. Most important among these convergences is the very fact of the shared organization around narrative, which chapter 2 explores in its historical context (and contingency).

Part 2: Knowing Law in Film   Here, with the historical and narrative-theoretical offerings of part 1 as foundation and backdrop, the focus turns to specific consideration of the presence of law and legal themes in film. This part includes the book's major statements of textual theory, centering around the thesis that films about law, because they are narratives about a narrative enterprise, may be understood as *reflexive.* Chapter 3 gives this argument context and contour by developing it in proximity to a consideration of the relevance of genre theory to the same body of films. This treatment examines the similarities and differences between a genre-based approach and the reflexivity-based theory under development here. As part of that examination, chapter 4 looks closely at the matter of history, as it relates to the process of theorizing about the presence of legal themes in particular films.

Part 3: Regimes of Writing   Marshaled under this banner are several essays dealing with the handling of the law-and-film relationship as it emerges in particular bodies of writing. In chapter 5, I explore the common ground of film and law with respect to analogy and metaphor. Theorists from both fields have liberally borrowed metaphors from each other, and here I look at examples of such cross-borrowings in connection with two themes, the *detective* and the *witness,* to see what happens in the course of a sustained and detailed examination of the metaphorical connections they suggest.

Chapter 6 offers a survey and analysis of written work by legal scholars having to do with film—including articles that use the plots and themes of particular films as points of departure for discussion of legal issues; that describe and reflect on the use of fiction film as a teaching device in the law school classroom; and that examine the position of film within the framework provided by related work in other interdisciplinary branches of legal scholarship. Although I originally envisioned this as a kind of research mop-up, it transpired that important issues are at stake in this area, for theory and for pedagogy, and that there is considerable room for commentary from the perspective of the discipline of film theory. (This chapter also provides a vehicle for introducing and addressing the law-and-literature movement, which has provided an intellectual home base for many legal writings on film.)

In chapter 7 I look at the commonplace but still curious phenomenon of probabilistic reasoning, fact-finding, and rhetoric in the texts of filmic response. This type of reasoning—namely, that which holds films accountable for a supposed accuracy and plausibility in the representation of social and historical data—has, among other things, a forensic quality reminiscent of the rhetoric and even the investigative strategies of legal process itself. Film criticism—and even everyday person-to-person evaluation of film—offers a striking example of a kind of subterranean crossover between the premises and practices of the filmic and legal regimes.

Part 4: Power, Prison, Pain   By way of uneasy conclusion, this part of the book introduces concerns that disturb whatever symmetry there might have been to the theories presented up to this point. Specifically, it offers a consideration of the matter of punishment—a part of legal process that does not necessarily fit easily into the framework provided but does raise some key questions. Also developed here are analyses of two films that revolve around the friction of incompatible or competing systems of justice and therefore stretch the boundaries of this book's argumentation: *A Question of Silence* and *The Last Wave.*

Filmography   Films cited throughout the book receive uneven amounts of attention, and some of those mentioned in passing are not always identified very fully. To compensate at least in part for this circumstance, I include at the end of the book a listing of all films mentioned in the text; each entry includes the title, director, country of origin, and year of release.

Notes

1. Among other law-film topics *not* under consideration here: copyright issues, censorship, and cameras in the courtroom. Cynthia Lucia shared with me an account of having been shown an orientation film when she was on jury duty—yet another piece of the endless law-and-film puzzle.

Part 1

Fundaments of Legal and Cinematic Narrative

1

Toward a Working Definition of Narrative

Narrative: A Provisional Master Term

At the most abstract level, the regimes of film and law may be said to traffic in symbolic representation. More concretely, they may be said to revolve around the constant production of probabilistic, linear stories (even if that production process itself is not always linear). Somewhere in the middle of this spectrum of specificity lies the notion of *narrative*, a term that has a foot in each of several camps of meaning and will serve here as a provisional master term for the characterization of the procedural overlap between law and film.

Narrative as a critical term has undergone considerable amounts of scrutiny, discussion, and debate. Entering into this debate is only useful here to the extent that it sets the stage for what follows—that is, for a consideration of the governance of legal and filmic practice by the received rules of narrative construction and of the role of narrativity itself as a kind of cultural and cognitive hub among whose spokes we may count the textual products of both film and law. Given the centrality of narrative to this project, and its history of less than consistent characterization in theoretical writings, it will be useful, I believe, to say something about it first.

What follows is not so much an attempt to resolve the issues behind the various debates as it is a bid for a working definition of narrative, in the form of a reasoned position statement. It may fairly be called a position statement (rather than, for instance, a survey of positions) because it proceeds from some already formed assumptions about narrative, or at least about what the central issues are, and with what priority they need to be introduced and addressed. Specifically, as will emerge below and remain in view throughout this book, I consider the question of verbal discourse—actual words, spoken or written, and/or the mental construction of propositional forms that will (or could) issue forth in actual words—to lie at the heart of narrative. This is not self-evident; there are plenty of theorists for whom "narrative" is a transcendent category, unconditional upon the medium in which it appears, neither more nor less itself in the presence or absence of natural language and verbal discourse. I will argue here against this medium-indifferent perspective on narrative, in part by examining what I view as the conundra encountered by theorists who have embraced it, and I will offer a working definition of narrative rooted in its rejection.

Tailoring the Term: Cloth or Clothes? Very broadly speaking, the term "narrative" lends itself to two usages, the distinction between which is roughly analogous to the distinction between the terms "cloth" and "clothes." To some extent, this distinction maps onto the difference between the notion of "narrative" and that of "a narrative." Narrative as cloth is a raw material, a phenomenon of representation, which may or may not find itself worked into a given form. By this light, for example, "Jesus wept" is narrative. But it is not *a* narrative— that is, a finished product with a beginning, a conflict, and a resolution.

I would suggest that both of these meanings, or levels of meaning, have their uses. It is important, in particular, not to lose sight of the first—that is, to recognize that attributes such as beginning and resolution represent, already, a kind of secondary articulation. Once we predicate specific story elements, the term "narrative" becomes too brittle to refer to the more raw, fluid thing that might also be called "narrative." We need a more "low-level," atomic term to describe, in effect, the fabric from which a narrative is constructed (just as we cannot replace all occurrences of the word "music" with "sonata"). "Jesus wept" is narrative because it is a present discourse (in this case, ink on a page) that symbolically (in this case, linguistically) represents an absent event. "Jesus wept" is thus narrative, in a way that, for instance, "two cups of flour" is not. The Gospel of St. Mark, on the other hand, is *a* narrative.

If a narrative is built up from narrative, it may also include nonnarrative elements, just as clothes may include not only cloth but also buttons and zippers. Indeed, as we attend to more and more nonnarrative elements (indexes, book covers, chapter titles, etc.), we slide gradually from a consideration of narrative to a consideration of textuality, in the sense set forth by Genette and others.

A Second Cut   Whatever view one takes of the term itself, the most vexed aspects of narrative are, first, its prolific behavior (its tendency to come at us in waves of repetition, reinstantiation, and, in general, serially manifested "versions" of itself) and, second, its promiscuity among media (the notion that "narrative" may be a phenomenon of writing, speech, film, ballet, painting, mime, and so forth). There are various matters at stake here that are worth teasing apart—matters of theoretical outlook as well as practice. But in the first instance, the prolificacy and the promiscuity really evaluate to the same thing: a detachment (at least a purported one) of the essence of the narrative from any of its particular material manifestations. To understand a ballet and a film, or a film and a *TV Guide* blurb, as versions of the "same thing" is to postulate a prior and noncontingent Thing; and both the proliferation of versions and the apparent indifference on the part of those versions to their medium of expression amount to cognitive inferences about the underlying properties of that Thing.

One way to handle this sprawling on the part of narrative is to acquiesce in it—to embrace as axiom the premise that a single narrative essence simply *has* the ability to travel from medium to medium, form to form, text to text, and yet remain itself in some essential way. Indeed, this is by far the best way to describe the observable *behavior* of narrative, and the way it is perceived and implemented by its practitioners. On the other hand, such a description—acquiescing, as it does, in the underpinnings of an idealistic and even metaphysical practice— poses problems for any narrative theory concerned with probing more deeply into those underpinnings.

Selective Demystification

In a watershed 1980 article, Barbara Herrnstein Smith takes exception to what she describes as "a lingering strain of naive Platonism" in narrative theory. "The sort of dualism to which I refer," writes Smith,

is conspicuous in the title of Seymour Chatman's recently published study, *Story and Discourse*. That doubling (that is, story *and* discourse) alludes specifically to a two-leveled model of narrative that seems to be both the central hypothesis and the central assumption of a number of narratological theories which Chatman offers to set forth and synthesize. The dualism recurs throughout his study in several other sets of doublet terms: "deep structure" and "surface manifestation," "content plane" and "expression plane," *"histoire"* and *"récit,"* *"fabula"* and *"sjuzet,"* and "signified" and "signifier."[1]

Smith goes on to argue for a consideration of the material, social, and historical specificity of everything—each thing—that might be called a "version" of a narrative, down to and including the sketchiest synopsis. "For any particular narrative," she suggests, "there is no single *basically* basic story subsisting beneath it but, rather, an unlimited number of other narratives that can be *constructed in response* to it or *perceived as related* to it."[2] Smith's starting point is the work of Chatman, and a closer examination of that work here will move us toward some of the key issues in the present consideration of the nature of narrative.

Chatman and the "Branches of a Tree"

Chatman's theoretical constructs in *Story and Discourse* reflect a classic "branches-of-a-tree" approach: narrative is a fundamental cultural practice that can equally be conducted in verbal form, theater, ballet, cartoon, film, painting, and so forth. What connects these branches to the tree is that they are all "narrative," somewhat in the way that steak, potato chips, and ice cream are all food.

Chatman goes one step beyond an essentialist comparison of narrative versions and applies the same reasoning to narrative-theoretical terms such as "duration," "pause," "stretch," and "description." Proceeding from the position that narrative is medium-independent, Chatman infers that a critical term applicable to a discursive practice in one medium's narratives will have an equivalent in the narratives of other media—and he implies the corollary, that if a single given term serves to label the practices of multiple media, those practices themselves may be understood as equivalent.

Consider Chatman's comments on duration and in particular on the technique he calls "stretch." "Duration," explains Chatman (following familiar arguments in narratology), "concerns the relation of the time it takes to read out the narrative to the time the story-events themselves lasted."[3] ("Read out" is intended here in the specialized sense of acceding to the deeper structure, the "story-level" of the narrative through the discourse, whatever medium it may happen to be in.) He enumerates all the possible permutations (less than, equal to, greater than) and gives commentary on and examples of each.

With regard to stretch, Chatman explains: "Here discourse-time is longer than story-time"[4]—that is, the time consumed in negotiating the narrative (book, film, or whatever) is longer than the time represented by the narrative. The difficulty of measuring discourse-time in literary texts is notorious: there is no predictable or consistent duration to the act of reading. Things are a little easier in the cinema, since under most circumstances we can quite precisely measure the running time of a film or filmic sequence. Already, then, it seems unlikely that a single phenomenon called "stretch" is going to manifest itself in any meaningfully similar way in the two media. But what Chatman does is to take as axiom the presumed equivalence of the concept "stretch" as between literary and filmic narratives and adduce comparative examples. "By 'overcranking'—that is, running the camera at a faster speed than its later projection—the cinema can manifest stretch in the well-known 'slow motion.'"[5] This is already problematic. (Does the dream sequence in *Los Olvidados* "stretch" "story-time"?) Chatman goes on to introduce literary examples of "stretch," including one that explores the relation between how long it takes to read a passage representing a character's mental processes and how long it presumably took to think them (as in Ambrose Bierce's "Occurrence at Owl Creek Bridge," where the hanging victim undergoes a protracted escape fantasy in the last moment before death).

The difficulty here—and, as a narratological examination, it is a kind of metadifficulty on the whole issue of comparing narratives from different media—is that the assumption of uniformity of meaning across multiple uses of the terminology ("stretch," in this case) obviates the establishment of any other, and perhaps more compelling, connection between the examples introduced. In other words, very little formally or experientially connects a slow-motion film sequence and a protracted stream-of-consciousness literary passage, except that they may both admit of being called "stretch." Beyond this terminological convergence, and in spite of it, it is difficult to see any further, critically meaningful connection between, for example, the slow-motion running of "The Six Million Dollar Man" (which indeed happens to signify that everything he does "bionically" is *accelerated*) and, say, the figure of "repetition" in the *nouveau roman*.

The next subcategory of duration, after stretch, is "pause": "story-time stops though the discourse continues, as in descriptive passages. Since narrative is essentially a temporal art, another discourse form takes over."[6] Examples from literature involve descriptions of scenes or situations without temporal progress, as well as devices such as that of a conversation contrived to allow a knowledgeable or expert character to introduce information into the story. Later, Chatman situates "set description" at the "weak" end of the spectrum of "overt narration."[7]

As for film, "the effect of pure description only seems to occur when the film actually 'stops,' in the so-called 'freeze-frame' effect (the projector continues, but all the frames show exactly the same image)." The example that follows is DeWitt's voice-over at the award ceremony at the beginning of *All about Eve*.[8]

Chatman also explains, however, that film by its nature partakes of a greater degree of *Bestimmtheit*, or specification, than verbal narrative in precisely the area of description: "cinematic narratives display an infinity of visual details (the color of the hero's shirt, the exact contours of the heroine's hairdo, the minutest architectural particulars of the house they enter). Such details can only be evoked by verbal narrative. Further, these words, in block descriptions, may arrest the story-time, which induces a sense of artifice and of a narrator's presence."[9]

But if by its very *Bestimmtheit* film always generates something that is the cinematic equivalent of literary "description," then what is the special place of the freeze-frame-plus-voice-over? And if the latter is equivalent to description passages in verbal narrative, is it also at the "weak" end of the spectrum of "overt" narration?[10] It begins to sound as if A > B > C > A.

The category of description thus also exhibits the problems of the matching of registers between the two media. These problems, as they arise here, affect Chatman's discussion of the unreliable narrator in film, in particular his example of the "lying flashback" in Hitchcock's *Stage Fright*.

It is characteristic of filmic narratology to go along with the verbal values assigned to filmic sequences as prompted by the diegesis of the film. The coinciding of the "knowledge" of a character who "tells" a flashback sequence seems to depend directly on the verbal distillation of the flashback: the issue of whether the character-narrator "knows" the harmonic progression of the music or the percentage of the screen taken up by a coffee cup falls by the wayside. Mismatches between character knowledge and flashback contents are recognized, but they generally have to do with units of speech: "He couldn't have known that" means "A verbal account of that could not have been among the things he said to the diegetic audience while we were watching the flashback." "Knowledge" means authority to verbalize and to be thought of as having verbalized.

Chatman's approach to the Hitchcock example follows this logic. And there is nothing "wrong" with it, since there is nothing "wrong" with concerning oneself with any unit of narrative measure in itself. But it results in difficulties for Chatman, because it points up further contradictions and crossed wires in his attempt to match up registers of narration and narratedness between filmic and verbal texts. Clearly he understands *Stage Fright*'s Johnnie as performing speech acts—specifically, lying. But "the camera" shows us the flashback. Now it has been established that the wealth of visual detail, the *Bestimmtheit* of film, is the equivalent of enormously detailed verbal description in the realm of verbal narrative. Johnnie is performing a verbal narrative. Does his speech therefore contain all (!) the details of the filmic flashback? If not—if, instead, the flashback can be measured in units of unheard but presumably relatively *unbestimmt* words—then why is any other filmic passage (which happens not to have a character-narrator) not also so interpretable and therefore *not* equivalent to detailed verbal description? But for Chatman the camera is the implied author, not the narrator.[11] So does the detail in the flashback come from the implied author? Then again, in a novel version it would come from the narrator, in whose words we read the flashback . . .

Although it may sound like a programmatic reductio ad absurdum, this last paragraph is in fact a diligent attempt to sort out the threads of Chatman's argument, an argument that suffers in almost direct proportion to the extent to which it tries to advance equivalences between filmic and verbal narrative discourses by giving their features and operations identical names. (Indeed, the best parts of the book are those in which cinema figures as an afterthought.) Furthermore, at the root of almost every instance of entanglement or contrivance lies some kind of privileging of the verbal, but it is never acknowledged. Thus, *Bestimmtheit*—defined in terms of what degree of verbal endeavor could replicate it in the written narrative text—has its place as a critical category in film only until a filmic character is posited as performing an *unbestimmt* verbal narrative act. Moreover, rarely is pride of place given to the filmic device: freeze-frames with voice-over are "description," but verbal descriptions are not referred to as "freeze-frames with voice-over." This problem is avoided sometimes by the use of noncommittal terms (like "stretch"), but these—aside from the problems they can cause, as suggested above—can be traced in many cases to a literary model or example. When, on the other hand, a literary passage, such as one from Nabokov's *Lolita*, is described as using "the montage-sequence technique," the cinema-derived appellation seems gratuitous and euphemistic—whereas the "problem" that the technique was "invented to solve" is that of communicating "summary," a supposedly even-handed but actually very literary term, in the cinema.[12]

The difficulty with this particular branches-of-a-tree reckoning with filmic and literary narrative is that it creates problems for itself by not confronting head-on some of the questions raised very readily in response to it—in the areas of verbalization, the exchange value of words and filmic sequences, and the shifts in registration and alignment of narrators and their position with regard to the word, all of which have so much bearing on the relation of the two narrative forms. My criticism of Chatman in these terms is not that he introduces the wrong issues but that he introduces them in the wrong order or at disparate levels of explicitness. The thesis that narrative is something that can inhabit various forms, and yet be found in detail to operate the same way in all of them, leaves us with a number of problems, already rendered virtually insoluble.

What Chatman runs aground on is the matter of *verbal abstraction*, here at the level of narratological terminology. As I will suggest below, it is also possible to run aground on the same thing at various other levels. In the aggregate, all of this concerns us because both law and film are saturated with verbal abstraction.

Bordwell, Constructivism, and the Struggle with the Word

In *Narration in the Fiction Film*, David Bordwell offers a different approach to the question of filmic narrativity, grounded in cognitive psychology and making use of the notion of "hypothesis-testing" as a unifying principle in the handling of the respondent's organizational and cognitive activities.

In the book's early chapters, Bordwell aligns himself with certain work in cognitive psychology by advancing a Constructivist account of filmic comprehension in which he argues that the spectator has an active, intelligent role in the construction of sense and meaning. This approach, Bordwell explains, in terms familiar from cognitive psychology, takes the construction of meaning as having a "bottom-up" and a "top-down" aspect; comprehension thus involves an encounter between sensory stimuli and mental activity and is never wholly determined by either one. "The spectator brings to the artwork expectations and hypotheses born of schemata, those in turn being derived from everyday experience, other artworks, and so forth. The artwork sets limits on what the spectator does."[13]

Since Bordwell rests much of his case on a Constructivist foundation, I would like to approach his work by way of a brief detour through another work that takes a kindred approach to a related topic, a look at which will provide us with—if not a really expansive context for Bordwell—at least one other text off of which to play his ideas. The work I have in mind is Irvin Rock's *Logic of Perception*. In this book, Rock argues that perception itself can be best understood as involving processes that very closely resemble those of intelligence; perception may therefore be studied as a cognitive rather than a purely reflexive process, one that involves problem solving. "My view [is] that perceptual processing is guided by the effort or search to interpret the proximal stimulus, i.e., the stimulus impinging on the sense organ, in terms of what object or event in the world it represents, what others have referred to as the 'effort after meaning.' In other words, the goal of processing is to arrive at a description of the outer object or event."[14]

Through the early chapters of the book, Rock draws out this notion of the description, which functions as a "propositional and abstract . . . correlate of the percept."[15] The case of form recognition, and in particular the question of left-right orientation, gives one illustration of the concept: "If we assume that what matters in the process of describing a figure as far as orientation is concerned is what regions are at the top, bottom, and sides and that, moreover, the sides are taken to be equivalent, then the description of a figure and its mirror image would be essentially alike. Thus if a *b* is 'a vertical straight line with a closed loop extending sideways at the bottom,' so too is a *d*."[16] Therefore, we recognize them as the same form.

Rock goes to some trouble to insist that the abstract "descriptions" he is proposing are in fact nonverbal, yet analogous in their own sphere to verbal hypothesizing in its sphere: the process of description "has the status of a hypothetical process which proceeds *as if* it conforms to the way in which we would consciously and verbally describe a figure.

Whatever the units or 'language' of such a description, many animal species and preverbal children must be capable of employing them."[17]

But the quotation marks lie uneasily about the word "language." Rock wrestles with the problem of natural language but never convincingly establishes that he has solved it. This is not only because *he* uses verbal language to point to the postulated nonverbal "language" of the perceptual "description" but in fact more because there is a curiously consistent correspondence between the success on the part of these descriptions in being chosen (or "preferred") by the perceptual apparatus and their proximity to verbal units. When, for example, experimental subjects have trouble recognizing an irregular geometrical form seen once in isolation and then among a group of similar but not identical forms, Rock traces the difficulty to categories of simplicity, complexity, and the consequentiality (or lack thereof) of parts of the whole. But one never escapes the impression that complexity for Rock *always* coincides with the effort it would take to describe the form *verbally*. Simple forms, it transpires, always manage to have few words attached to them: square, Christmas tree, circle, map of Africa, and so forth. In spite of the persuasiveness of his hypothesis that perception involves processes like those of cognition, Rock never convincingly puts to rest the objection that the supposedly nonverbal "description" he postulates does in fact rise and fall with the pull of actual, speakable words, nor the impression that the process of abstraction into recognition performed by the sensory agency runs inside the grooves etched by natural language.[18]

At the outset, Bordwell is explicit and emphatic in his refusal for his theory of something he calls "verbal activity" as a means of accounting for the cognition of filmic narrative, an approach whose exponents (he names Colin MacCabe and Christian Metz in particular) "have notably ignored the spectator. When the perceiver is discussed, it is usually as the victim or dupe of narrational illusion-making."[19] In redressing this problem, Bordwell puts aside linguistic models in favor of Constructivist approaches to perception and cognition; he thus situates himself as an intellectual cousin to Rock (and likewise traces his ancestry to Helmholtz).

What exactly is it that Bordwell rejects? "It will come as no surprise," he states,

that I do not treat the spectator's operations as necessarily modeled upon linguistic activities. . . . It is by no means clearly established that human perception and cognition are fundamentally determined by the processes of natural language; indeed, much psycholinguistic evidence runs the other way. . . . For such reasons, I do not call the spectator's comprehension "reading" a film. . . . Viewing is synoptic, tied to the time of the text's presentation; it does not require translation into verbal terms.[20]

It is not entirely clear what Bordwell means by "synoptic" here—perhaps that viewing time and textual manifestation are coterminal on both ends (which only means that a thorough consideration of the spectator's position in the cinema will have to attend to something more inclusive than "viewing"). But the most striking action of this passage is the collapsing into one school of critical approach—for the purpose of its rejection—linguistic models of cognition, "language of film" theories, and concern with materially manifest verbal activity. There is no distinction made here between questions that are in fact widely separate from each other, such as: Does film syntax function in ways analogous to that of verbal language? Do people only know the world through its division into linguistic units? and—significantly—What can we say about the link between the knowable facts about practices of verbal recounting and the very narrativity of filmic narrative? In fact, Bordwell applies the brand of "verbal activity" to any term referring to natural language in any capacity, declares linguistics unhelpful, and thereby opens a chasm in his theory that will never be convincingly bridged. Putting aside all head-on reckoning with the significance of actual verbal activity is in no sense a necessary concomitant of departing from a Metzian approach. By collapsing the two, Bordwell prejudices the fortunes of his own experiment in abstaining from linguistic models.

Understood within a Constructivist framework, Bordwell suggests, film viewing would involve several factors. On the "bottom-up" side are those physical aspects of the film that induce the effects of apparent motion and image constancy (as well, it is claimed, as color).[21] "Top-down" contributions involve "prior knowledge and experience. . . . Everything from recognizing objects and understanding dialogue to comprehending the film's overall story utilizes previous knowledge."[22] Then there is "the material and structure of the film itself," of which Bordwell takes a rather benign view: "The narrative film is so made as to encourage the spectator to execute story-constructing activities. The film presents cues, patterns, and gaps that shape the viewer's application of schemata and the testing of hypotheses."[23]

Even at the stage of introducing these factors, and even in explaining that they are in fact interactive, Bordwell initiates a process of vertical integration that only confirms the earlier sighting of a chasm in his theory at the very point where one might interpose a consideration of verbal activity. There is, in effect, no link offered between the quasi-neurological, dissective discussion of the perception of apparent motion and the fully participatory description of "events," "temporal sequence," and "story": the question of what makes it *possible* for all these cues, patterns, and gaps to be narrative—to be received, studied, disseminated as narrative—disappears into the folds of the shroud covering the linguistic analogy, whence it never reappears, save as a specter, uninvited.

The principal means of this vertical integration is the notion of hypothesis testing.[24] Initially a vehicle for understanding spectator activity, hypothesis testing takes the reins, ending up as a runaway concept that too rapidly ties together many levels of cognition: suddenly, we are reading about the characters in *Rear Window* testing hypotheses at the diegetic level. The journey from perception psychology to diegetic autonomy has been made smooth by some metaphorically expansive terms, but its underpinnings have not been thoroughly explained.

Bordwell's "hypotheses" behave very much like Rock's "descriptions," and they provoke very similar questions: If the theoretical model on offer does *not* predicate some kind of packaging of nonverbal information into verbal form, one continually asks, then what does it predicate? How can one tell that it is nonverbal? If it *is* ultimately nonverbal, but has been trained through the centuries to subordinate itself to words—to set its own nodes of significance at exactly the same points as natural language—should that not be taken seriously into account?

That the chasm in the theory owes its existence, however ironically, to precisely the spectral presence of verbal activity becomes particularly clear in succeeding chapters, but a "symptomatic reading" of Bordwell's early handling of the problem of filmic narrativity also brings it to light. "Comprehending a narrative," he argues, "requires assigning it some coherence. At a local level, the viewer must grasp character relations, lines of dialogue, relations between shots, and so on. More broadly, the viewer must test the narrative information for consistency: does it hang together in a way we can identify? For instance, does a series of gestures, words, and manipulations of objects add up to the action sequence we know as 'buying a loaf of bread'?"[25]

It is difficult to see how this passage offers an *alternative* to the hypothesis that filmic narrativity depends on the processing of miscellaneous input into words. This difficulty in Bordwell's argument (which cannot be written off as a necessity of the hardships of writing about film) does not disappear. In fact, when Bordwell later chooses to discuss filmic narrative in terms of the formalist categories of fabula and syuzhet, the unacknowledged dependence on verbal activity only deepens. It continues to take the form of a tug-of-war (as in Rock) but is never resolved.

In the fabula/syuzhet terminological pair, *fabula* refers to an underlying—and ideal—commonality of content (roughly, "the story"), while *syuzhet* refers to the narrative properties and ordering of any given material instantiation of the fabula. Thus, in the case of a flashback sequence, for example, the ordering of events in the syuzhet (present followed by past) reverse those of the fabula. Initially, Bordwell has this to say on the subject: "The fabula is thus a pattern which perceivers of narratives create through assumptions and inferences. It is the developing result of picking up narrative cues, applying schemata, framing and testing hypotheses. Ideally, the fabula can be embodied in a verbal synopsis, as general or as detailed as circumstances require."[26] Elaborating the point, Bordwell continues: "At a gross level, the same fabula could be inferred from a novel, a film, a painting, or a play. Thus one difficulty of enunciative theories—the forced analogy between linguistic categories and nonverbal phenomena—vanishes. . . . contrary to what some writers believe, the fabula/syuzhet distinction does not replicate the *histoire/discours* distinction held by enunciation theories."[27]

The fabula/syuzhet duplet is among those attacked by Smith for its Platonism, and the fact that Bordwell has recourse to it while attempting to avoid verbal models certainly does not figure as evidence *against* a theory of verbal activity as a structuring principle of filmic narrativity. Moreover, while it may be argued that the fabula per se, while ideal, is not necessarily verbal (a questionable claim), Bordwell's case is not helped either by his invocation of the practice of verbal synopsis in connection with it. Of the many items on the agenda of *Narration in the Fiction Film,* that of denying a role to verbal activity is mortally stricken by all this unacknowledged tarrying at the brink of the paraphrase. Thus, Bordwell's contribution to an understanding of the workings of narrative film must be considered apart from the fate of his programmatic refusal of the word.

Narrativity and the Word

In somewhat different ways, these passages by Bordwell and Chatman exemplify what Smith is justifiably concerned about: namely, the tendency of narrative theorists, who arguably should be taking a step back from narrative intuition and practice, to take the metaphysics of narrative at face value. But there is something further that Bordwell and Chatman have in common and that Smith does not address as fully as I will here. Chatman and Bordwell both run aground on the same thing: the centrality of *verbal* discourse and paraphrase to the supposedly medium-indifferent practice of narrative. With Chatman, again, we are on a metalevel; it is not the verbality of the narrative itself that comes into play but that of the terminology: the word "stretch" functions, with regard to Chatman's various examples, very much as the phrase "buying a loaf of bread" does for Bordwell—that is, as a lexical common denominator, the very entity the two theorists wish to claim does not exist.

These isolated and even rarified examples take us to something of the greatest general importance for a consideration of narrative: namely, the role of language and verbal abstraction. On the one hand, Smith is right to warn us that, while narrative versions seem to behave as if they were all equally derived from a synoptic primary version that can be expressed verbally, the verbal synopsis is essentially just another version, with its own materiality, context, and purpose. On the other hand, Smith's argument leaves a void. She advocates seeing all versions in succession, as a sort of row of utterances. This is a useful corrective to the idealistic view that content travels from form to form; but the fact is that narrative, as a cultural practice, does operate as Chatman and Bordwell suggest—less as a succession of utterances and more as a kind of hub-and-spoke apparatus, where the hub is the ostensible essence (content, story, fabula) and the spokes are the various versions in various media (form, discourse, syuzhet).

As theorists of narrative, we need a way to allude to and describe this hub-and-spoke behavior on the part of narrative, even if that behavior is very ideal and metaphysical, and even—especially—if we want to be able to say something more about it than that it is naïve. This is where language and verbal paraphrase are, in one form or another, indispensable. The key, however, is to recognize that the "hub" is not the actual verbal synopsis but rather the linguistic potential of the narrative. In other words, when we read, see, or hear narrative, we are left with—

among other impressions—a kind of verbal or preverbal trace; we are, from that point on, able *and authorized* to retell or re-present the narrative. This may mean summarizing a movie to a friend, writing a screenplay based on a short story, or spreading a rumor. Whatever we end up doing (or not doing) with a given narrative, at some point in its life the narrative will have passed through a verbal phase.

This is, in part, an inductive argument; quite simply, I have never seen any convincing counterevidence about the nonverbal nature of narrative that does not run aground on the matter of dependence on language. Beyond (or alongside) the inductive evidence, there are two ways to pursue this argument. One is on a cognitive basis. A cognitive argument would revolve around the idea that mental representations of narrative are essentially verbal, that in some sense narrativity itself depends on the process of linguistic representation. Of course, there are aspects of a ballet that do not lend themselves to verbal paraphrase: qualities of grace; details of movements that may relate to a narrative but cannot be mapped precisely onto a verbal version; in the case of some ballets perhaps extensive lengths of dance that are not in any sense telling a story. One might argue, however—and I tend to believe this—that such things are not, strictly speaking, narrative. They may be characteristics of something that is also a narrative, but they do not themselves account for narrativity as such.

The second way to document the centrality of language to narrative is empirically. Whatever the truth behind the debate over cognitive processes—that is, whether our private mental representations of narrative are verbal *or not*—there is a cultural fact that may or may not harmonize with the cognitive theory but that in any case does not depend on that theory: namely, that we do, in fact, verbalize narratives, exchange nonverbal for verbal narrative all the time, and live in a culture saturated with verbal synopsis. If this is the result, in part, of the pragmatics of narrative practice (it's hard to write a screenplay without a synopsis; it's hard to follow an opera without knowing the story; etc.), it is nonetheless the case that narratives, in nonverbal as well as verbal media, tend at least to pass through a verbal phase at some point in their life cycles. When someone asks us to recount the plot of a movie, we do not dance it out. Narrative medium is not a matter of indifference— and the fact that literature is verbal, and that we don't want to privilege literature, may have worked to obscure the fact that verbal activity (mental or otherwise) is the lingua franca of narrative. We certainly tend to see the ballet as the "real" thing and the printed synopsis as an adjunct to it—convenient, but not, in any deep sense, necessary. And if a narrative adapts a historical story, we see the history as "real" and the narrative as a gloss—and any short synopsis as a kind of trimming. Certainly the movie summaries in *TV Guide* do not substitute for the experience of seeing movies. Yet, in a sense, *they do;* at some level, *TV Guide* blurbs do function, or behave, as occupants of the narrative space of the movies they summarize. Verbal expression, in this regard, is the common currency of narrative.

There is thus a kind of exchange value in operation, a substitution of relatively brief verbal synopses for more attenuated narrative forms. It is important to remember, however, that this does not mean that the verbal synopsis actually is the ideal, essential core of the narrative, any more than a full-fledged novel is.

Logomorphism: A Metaphysical Truce

Other than the disagreement about the role of natural language in the processes in question, the direction in which I am moving here has a lot in common with the Constructivist approaches discussed above. Both are concerned with narrative cognition as an encounter between external stimuli and cognitive processes, allowing for shiftings of the balance in either direction.[28] Bordwell and Rock both recognize a process by which cognition organizes itself around certain nodes; encounters with data, filmic and otherwise, resolve themselves into patterns of core-and-residuum.

In fact, my model of narrativity might very well be described as one of "hypothesis testing" or "solution preference"; and while I shall not lean too heavily on these terms, I do not flinch from associating them with the argument under development here. That argument, after all, amounts to the claim that a narrative, whether or not it originates in words, functions as a series of obstacles that a verbal paraphrase has to negotiate. On this construction, a successful (i.e., lucid, cogent) paraphrase fills the role of something like a "preferred solution" in the course of hypothesis testing.

I shall not expand specifically on these affinities as such; but they do point the way directly to a further elaboration of the theory under consideration in this chapter.

Let us return at this point to image naming as a starting point for the apprehension of filmic narrative. Image naming involves a kind of epistemological archery: faced with something material and visual, we target "what is" in the picture and name it. This process—however practiced, innocent, self-evident, and so forth—*always* entails the falling away of an infinite number of equally defensible choices. One *could have said* (or could have been brought to the readiness to say), "There is a gray parallelogram partially occluded by a tapering surface whose color undergoes a gradual change," instead of, "There is a decanter on a table." The former description, however willfully opaque or bizarre, is as correct as the latter (though one might might far more confidently bet on the likelihood of actually hearing the latter in the course of a verbal account of a film). Descriptions of the former kind may be termed "eccentric," not only by the standards of common sense, but in the specific sense (pursuing the archery metaphor) that they lie outside the "bull's-eye"; that is, they are not "target responses."

If an image can yield an infinite number of such eccentric readings, then the number that an entire film can generate is infinity raised to some unthinkable power. Not only can we say "A courtroom just vanished" instead of "The hero told his story on the stand and it was shown in flashback," but we can break the courtroom down into a million little parts (for each frame, in fact) and describe each one in compulsive detail. It would be counterproductive to look at the less "eccentric" utterance—the one that seems to find the target of the content of the film—as "upwardly integrative" of any of the others. They are all, in theory, equally available and equally correct; the placement of the bull's-eye is a matter of convention.[29]

Strictly based on the exercise of finding words that accurately relate what one has apprehended from the sensory data of a film, then, one might come up with any of an infinite number of possible "solutions" to the text, just as, for Rock, the perceptual apparatus constructs "descriptions" out of a miscellany of sensory data. How does this figure in the question of filmic narrativity? I would assign it a very central place; in fact, I would argue that the task of the competent respondent to narrative film can be defined in large part as the construction of a "solution" or "description" *that can stand on its own as a coherent, relatable, usable verbal narrative.* The spectator encounters a vast succession of moving, permeable targets, each with a relatively small bull's-eye and a much larger region of eccentricity, and must find a course that hits as many bull's-eyes as possible. The successful trajectory through the film is that which ongoingly avoids the marginal or eccentric response and thus cumulatively shapes itself into or around the coherent verbal paraphrase. In this manner, *narrative film* establishes and employs the preconditions of *filmic narrativity.*

It is this cumulative verbal response, incessantly chosen and rechosen out of infinite alternatives, that figures in the present context as the hypothesis does for Bordwell or the description for Rock. Like both of those terms, it suggests nodes of attraction around which cognition and recognition cluster. Unlike theirs, however, the cumulative verbal response's nodes of attraction are unabashedly verbal. At the same time, and by the same token that I have had occasion to speak of recountability as much as of recounting, the verbal nature of this "response" does not depend completely on material instantiation—the generation of audible speech—but also resides, partly, in the potential for materiality. The cumulative verbal response to a film need not take the form of spoken words or even an inwardly audible running commentary. It may take such forms; but more fundamentally, and more exactly, it consists of the readiness to speak, the authority to recount the film. It concatenates the nodes of significance around which the film must organize itself, nodes that *are* coincident with accessible words. This once-and-future narrative, to which I would attribute the very *possibility* of filmic narrativity, I shall refer to as the *logomorph.*[30]

The negotiation of the text by the derivation of the logomorph represents a *process* by which we perform a series of successful meetings with "bull's-eyes"; the task of the narrative film (in this connection, at least) is to dispose itself so that the likelihood of such "hits" is maximized and the likelihood of "eccentric" readings reduced. Obviously a given film can produce a harvest of what at least seem to be wildly variant readings, but I would argue that if one begins from the assumption that *any* eccentric reading, as defined above, can logically be placed on the same footing as any other reading, then it becomes necessary to account for the relatively great convergence of observable response, as well as for diversity. Logomorphic response to narrative film proceeds through clusters of consensus, peaks of a succession of cognitive bell curves, with less likely or less frequent readings falling away at the sides. The successful narrative film in this regime leaps as cleanly as possible from one peak to the next.[31]

Whether we take it as an irreducible cognitive matter or as a social practice that at least finds no resistance from the mind, something is going on with language here—it really is serving a "hub" purpose. I want to preserve the major points of Smith, but I also want to acknowledge that narrative behaves according to these metaphysical assumptions. My compromise or truce is the notion of the "logomorphic" (borrowed from Metz and Morin, but freely adapted). The idea is that narrative, in whatever medium, at some point along the way resolves itself into language or is safeguarded (i.e., represented or remembered) in a form that either is language or can be made into language. To say, for instance, that a ballet is "logomorphic" is not to say that it is a verbal art form but, rather, that—to the extent it is narrative—it has a verbal, propositional infrastructure: *we can tell it.*

This question—the relation among events and their versions—becomes very important in both legal and cinematic narrative practice, once we look at those practices in a context that embraces not only what is on the screen and what is in the court transcript but the whole chain of processes involved and the motives and reasons behind them. The point of legal procedure, basically, is to go from a miscellany of events (crimes) to a verdict—that is, to filter history through discourse, ultimately distilling it to a single word.

Narrative: A Working Definition

I would like to leave a number of these questions open-ended, but here is at least a tentative working definition of narrative: *the logomorphic representation of absent events in present discourses.* This is both a working definition and a position statement—the latter, because it is not neutral on some debatable points. Specifically, I shall adhere to the tenet that *narrativity itself* depends on logomorphism (i.e., that whatever the medium at hand—and however "visual" that medium may be—verbal recountability is a necessary, though not sufficient, condition of narrativity); and, importantly, to the hypothesis that narrative's referent events (however photorealistic and/or politically potent may be the acts of their public representation) can only be, and always are, *absent.*

Notes

1. Barbara Herrnstein Smith, "Narrative Versions, Narrative Theories," *Critical Inquiry* 7.1 (Autumn 1980): 213.

2. Ibid., 221.

3. Seymour Chatman, *Story and Discourse: Narrative Structure in Fiction and Film* (Ithaca, N.Y.: Cornell University Press, 1978), 67–68.

4. Ibid., 72.

5. Ibid.

6. Ibid., 74.

7. Ibid., 219. See also note 10.

8. Ibid., 75.

9. Ibid., 222–23.

10. An example of a strong form of overt narration for Chatman is that which summarizes time rather than describing space and objects while time is suspended. Temporal summary, Chatman argues, displays more strongly the presence of a narrator (222–25).

11. See Chatman's discussion of *Stage Fright* and his remarks on the unreliable narrator and the implied author in film (235–37).

12. See Chatman's remarks on summary, montage, and the example of "montage" from *Lolita* (68–70).

13. David Bordwell, *Narration in the Fiction Film* (Madison: University of Wisconsin Press, 1985), 32.

14. Irvin Rock, *The Logic of Perception* (Cambridge: MIT Press, 1983), 16.

15. Ibid., 52.

16. Ibid., 51.

17. Ibid.

18. Rock discusses simplicity and complexity throughout the book, but see especially chapter 3 and the diagrams and reports of experiments under the headings of "Orientation" and "Complexity" (48–57).

19. Bordwell, 30.

20. Ibid.

21. Ibid., 32–33.

22. Ibid.

23. Ibid., 33.

24. Bordwell introduces this concept on p. 37 and discusses it often throughout the book. He draws specifically on Meir Sternberg, *Expositional Modes and Temporal Ordering in Fiction* (Baltimore: Johns Hopkins University Press, 1978).

25. Bordwell, 34.

26. Ibid., 49.

27. Ibid., 51.

28. See David A. Black, "Cinematic Realism and the Phonographic Analogy," *Cinema Journal* 26.2 (Winter 1987): 39–50, esp. pp. 47–49, for a more extensive example of my own inclination toward graphic models of spectatorship as involving an encounter between text and psyche—in this case, based on Freud's model of progressive and regressive perception.

29. This "target" model represents my own coming to terms with what Chatman labels *Bestimmtheit*.

30. Metz takes up from Gilbert Cohen-Séat the notion of the "logomorphism" of film. While my use of the term represents something of a recoining and an investiture with new designs of connotation, the language used by Metz in this connection is certainly of interest here: "Narrativity and logomorphism. It is as if a kind of induction current were linking images among themselves, *whatever one did*, as if the human mind (the spectator's as well as the filmmaker's) were incapable of not making a connection between two successive images" (*Film Language: A Semiotics of the Cinema*, trans. Michael Taylor [New York: Oxford University Press, 1967], 93). See also Gilbert Cohen-Séat, *Essai sur les principes d'une philosophie du cinéma* (Paris: Presses Universitaires de France, 1958), 128.

31. Certain narrative devices in film may be said to involve a sort of inverted logomorphic process, shifting *from* story-space speech or writing *to* filmic representation. A fully enacted flashback may be set as equivalent to an elided, verbally delivered speech on the part of a character or to the pages of a journal that dissolve into it; and it is not rare for discussions of such structures to favor the verbal paradigm, in the sense of following the film's prompt to assign a verbal value to the filmic sequence. (Film reception in general thus agrees at this point with the kind of film narratology expounded by Chatman and others.) Questions about the narrator's knowledge, the effect of the absent speech on its diegetic auditors, and so forth, are accordingly considered in a manner that handles the embedded filmic sequence as if it in fact had been spoken. Thus we do not feel obliged to wonder what the jury thought of a certain crane shot, or, in Welles's *Citizen Kane*, how Thompson, upon perusing Thatcher's journal, reacted to the placement of Agnes Moorehead in the composition. The logomorphic response of the spectator to the enacted sequence has the status of a sort of available twin of the unavailable diegetic verbal text that the film has chosen to abbreviate. One may therefore say that in such cases the logomorph doubly "targets" the flashback sequence: first, as it targets the filmic narrative in general; and second, on behalf of the missing verbal text, thus performing its own and the film's job of assigning words to "what is" shown, allowing an enormous number of alternate, equally defensible accounts to fall away.

2

Law and Film as Narrative Regimes

Narrative Regimes in Parallel

Setting out to describe law and film as narrative regimes "in parallel" is a bit like the process of introducing opponents in a boxing match while they are still in their respective corners. The analogy fails, perhaps, in point of antagonism and ill will. But it holds in two senses: first, that it is possible—that is, one can say, usefully, a fair amount along the lines of "Film, as narrative regime, operates thus" and "Law, as narrative regime, operates thus," before and outside of any direct encounter between the two; and second, that such parallel observations, in the absence of encounter, are distinctly by way of warm-up, rather than main event.

Indeed, defending the parallel arguments that film is a narrative regime and law is a narrative regime might be as simple as directing the reader to the courtroom and the movie theater. Plenty has been written about narrative film, film and narrative, law and narrative, and related topics; and plenty of that writing has involved disagreement and debate. I know of no denial, however, of the basic fact that narrative activity takes place in the realms of cinematic and legal process. In that respect—and if one takes the term "narrative regime" to reflect merely the presence of narrative, the commission, on institutional time, of acts of narrating—then there is hardly an argument to be made.

Of course, that nonargument is in many ways the touchstone of this book. I do not wish to be disloyal to it; but, equally, I do wish to explore its ramifications.

Law   To judge by the orientation of most of the meaningful debate concerning the matter of law as narrative regime, what is chiefly at stake is not the question of whether or not the various role-players in the legal system tell stories (which they do) but, rather, the role that narrative plays with respect to the further stakes of legal process and legal *power.*

The relation between legal procedure and narrative has been documented, written about, interpreted, and troubleshot from a number of perspectives and in a number of ways. One very lucid and convincing account of the role played by narrative, or storytelling, in Anglo-American law is provided by W. Lance Bennett and Martha S. Feldman in *Reconstructing Reality in the Courtroom:* "The interpretive powers of stories take on special significance in the courtroom. The overriding judgmental tasks in a trial involve constructing an interpretation for the defendant's alleged activities and determining how that interpretation fits into the set of legal criteria that must be applied to the defendant's behavior. . . . There are several characteristics of stories that make them suitable frameworks of legal judgment."[1]

The authors focus on the *functionality* of narrative within a regime of power—without taking the false step of inferring that narrative is the cause and power is the result. For Bennett and Feldman, the power of the adjudicatory process is indisputable, as is the presence of narrative in Anglo-American legal process. Their argument obviates the question of whether storytelling per se has ethical or political valence and focuses instead on describing the position of narrative practices within the regime of law. There are plenty of aspects of legal practice and procedure that are not narrative and are not aspects of narrative. But law does involve narrative—and narratives—and stories. It is also powerful—in sum, a powerful regime that involves, that *deploys,* narrative.

This may, indeed, be all the proof we need that narrative is powerful in itself. But it also may not be such proof, and it need not be so taken. To put it another way: as much as narrative happens to serve an instrumental function within a regime of power, there is, too, a *difference* between narrative and power and a difference between narrative and law—both of those differences being greater (though, surprisingly, sometimes harder to see) than the difference between law and power.

Bennett and Feldman see this, I believe. But not all theorists do—at least, not all theorists think all other theorists do. Instructive lessons on the urgency of not actually *equating* law and storytelling may be found—at the cost of putting a particular cart before its horse—in the writings of those legal scholars who have raised objections to the tenets and interpretive strategies of the so-called law-as-literature movement.[2] Such responses tend not to deny that there are narratives and stories at hand in the discourses of law but rather to suggest that the study of law as storytelling, literature, and/or narrative misses the point: namely, the power of the law. As Robin West argues in the oft-cited article "Adjudication Is Not Interpretation: Some Reservations about the Law-as-Literature Movement":

> The analogue of law to literature, . . . although fruitful, has carried legal theorists too far. Despite a superficial resemblance to literary interpretation, adjudication is not primarily an interpretive act of either a subjective or objective nature; adjudication, including constitutional adjudication, is an imperative act. Adjudication is in form interpretive, but in substance it is an exercise of power in a way which truly interpretive acts, such as literary interpretation, are not. Adjudication has far more in common with legislation, executive orders, administrative decrees, and the whimsical commands of princes, kings and tyrants than it has with other things we do with words, such as create or interpret novels. Like the commands of kings and the dictates of a majoritarian legislature, adjudication is imperative. It is a command backed by state power. No matter how many similarities adjudication has with literary linguistic activities, this central attribute distinguishes it. If we lose sight of the difference between literary interpretation and adjudication, and if we do not see that the difference between them is the amount of power wielded by the judiciary as compared to the power wielded by the interpreter, then we have either misconceived the nature of interpretation, or the nature of law, or both.[3]

In drawing attention to the question of judicial power, West characterizes that power as the difference between law and literature, which may be the case but does not mean that law is not centered around narrative. In fact, the idea of "the difference" opens another avenue of trouble; after all, if the difference between adjudication and cooking were that judges who cooked were allowed, when the pie came out of the oven, to send a randomly chosen person to prison, then we would do well to focus not on the triviality or inadequacy of cooking to the task of administering justice but on the fact that cooking—trivial in itself or not—had been elevated to a very high place and assigned, without any other changes to itself, a very powerful role.

This is precisely the point of looking at law as a cultural regime: to focus on formulating a statement of the *role* of narrativity and fabulation in legal process—not to deny that it is there, and not to assume that it is a subset or tendril of something else whose traits it has inherited wholesale (e.g., literature).

Both the similarities and the differences between law and literature (and, ultimately, between law and film) can be discerned by looking at them as regimes, in each of which various practices play various roles. Narrative theory is basically a regime of reading and responding. Law is basically a regime of actions and consequences. I do not mean by this that consequences—that is, punishments—necessarily fit the actions— that is, crimes. I mean, rather, that the skeletal framework of the legal regime consists of the action-consequence relation.

Reading and responding are things that begin and end with texts. Historically, many of those texts have proven to be narrative (though not all—let us not forget poetry and the middle ground of theater). In the case of law, *neither* of the polar, skeletal terms of the regime—neither crime nor punishment—is textual.[4] Whatever role textuality, narrative, storytelling, and literary critical practices play in the law, they play between the bookends, so to speak. Narrativity thus stands in a different relation to the structuring pillars of the regimes of law and literature.

This does not mean that narrativity does not play a part, nor does it put any restrictions on how important that part may be. Indeed, precisely what is disconcerting about the saturation of legal process with stories, narratives, and interpretations that *do* closely resemble literary responses is that something so weighty could in fact be conducted in an arena having so much in common with something like literature. In other words, one may, as West warns, trivialize or divert attention from the power of the law by being drawn only to its literary qualities. On the other hand, one might draw useful attention to the fact, if it is a fact, that law, though incredibly important, allows itself to operate by principles not radically different from those governing literary response. In other words, the argument that "adjudication is interpretation" (and related arguments) might be met with a response like, "Law is too weighty to be understood through techniques and processes that, while acceptable in their place, are rhetorical, formal, and literary rather than truth-engaged or political"—or, on the other hand, it might be met with, "Law, such a weighty thing, admits of understanding as narrative or literature—isn't that scary?"

To some extent, this is a semantic issue: if we invest "narrative" (or "literature" or "literary theory") with semantic properties of triviality, then those properties travel with the word. It seems to me that this is more the issue than the question of whether anything we can call "narrative" or "a story" occurs in the course of legal practice. Moreover, it is, beyond a certain point, a somewhat fruitless path. It is reminiscent of the argument that chimpanzees "use tools," an argument I have seen propounded on the basis of the fact that some chimpanzees were observed using a leaf to scoop food out of a tree hollow.[5] If we invest "using tools" with all the associations it has for humans, then the sight of a chimp using a leaf opens a floodgate of revisionist chimpanzee epistemology. If, however, we posit that "there are tools, and then there are tools," the sense of zoological revolution becomes a lot less forceful.

I have proposed that narrative is logomorphic—that is, the temporal and material persistence of (verbal or nonverbal) narratives and their versions has to do with words. Coming full circle, it remains to say something about the logomorphism of legal narrative. Like literature, storytelling, and film, logomorphism is not synonymous with narrative, but it is a condition of it and it does overlap with it. In other words, for every given narrative act, there are aspects that are nonlogomorphic and therefore nonnarrative; and there are, often, logomorphic aspects that are, though logomorphic, also nonnarrative. In the case of law, it seems to me that the power West and others draw attention to, as a caution against the possible formalistic excesses of actually equating law with narrative and/or narrative theory, is precisely that which escapes logomorphism. We can describe, tell, or narrate, for example, the sequence of events culminating in someone's being tortured to death in the electric chair. However, the suffering and death themselves are not, per se, narrative—not at all, not even to the extent that a judicial opinion might be said to "be," or even be like, a work of literary interpretation. In other words, if law is a regime that is heavily saturated with narrative and can be at least provocatively explored as a web of narrative acts and interpretations, nonetheless there lies something outside of narrative: the power of law, which, as things stand, arises as a consequence of narrative.

At the same time, it seems to me that there is logomorphism in law even where there is not narrative. It is the job of legal discourses to provide the passage between—or, perhaps, the glue that binds—actions and consequences. Actions, after taking place but before becoming the ostensible grounds for consequences, are subjected to logomorphism and/ or narrativity. Specifically, the actions eventuate in a *verdict*—that is, in a short, logically irreducible (if not always logical), logomorphic (in fact, verbal) pronouncement. The verdict is part of the story, but as such it is not narrative. Narrative is a tissue of change; a verdict is a celebration of stasis. In the rendering of the verdict, law escapes narrative, but it embraces logomorphism in its most distilled, potent form.

Film   The argument that film operates as a narrative regime can probably be made, if it needs making, by walking through a video store, opening a newspaper, or simply living in virtually any film-productive culture—certainly ours. In other words, films tell stories. The coefficient of narrativity per viewing hour is extremely high. When we go to the movie theater or rent a video, we expect a story. We may expect things other than a story, or more than one story, but at the very least— and very consistently over the vast majority of such transactions—we expect a story. We do not expect, for instance, a hundred minutes of scratched leader, nor abstract geometrical shapes gliding across the screen. We expect narrative.[6]

Film's narrativity has sparked an almost unchartable amount of commentary and criticism, as have various subtypes of filmic narrative and large numbers of specific narrative films. Here, I would like to maintain the focus by following two of the major threads that emerged in the course of looking at the matter of law as narrative regime: namely, the question of what lies *outside* of narrative in any given case (e.g., power in the case of law); and the role of logomorphism in the regime overall. Once the comparative framework is fully established, later sections will probe more deeply into particular aspects of legal and filmic narrative.

If films indeed tell stories, it also holds that the stories told by films get told as well by nonfilms, both orally and in print. We might attend a screening of Hitchcock's *Vertigo*, or we might encounter the sentence "A detective gets put through the wringer" in *TV Guide*.[7] In some sense, these are both *Vertigo*—at least, one is *Vertigo* and one is a kind of (tiny) narrative placeholder for it. The key point here is that somewhere along the line this mininarrative—despite its appointment to the task of standing in for the film in an ink-and-paper context—has branched away from *Vertigo*. In short, they *differ*, and that difference is formal, material, graphic, even narrative. It is also a difference between the presence and absence of *pleasure*.

Pleasure in film, like power in law, is that which lies beyond narrativity in a narrative regime. Pleasure can of course be derived from the narrative, but it is not limited to that derivation. The absence of pleasure in something like "A detective gets put through the wringer" is an important index of this—particularly important in light of the rather weighty role assigned to such synopses (if it is even that), summaries, and other retellings. Moreover, the absence of pleasure is a different thing here from the presence of *dis*pleasure. We do not react with pleasure to the "story" told by *TV Guide*, but, because no expectation of pleasure operates, we also do not experience displeasure.[8]

Displeasure, in the regime of film, attaches (or can attach) to exactly the same things that pleasure attaches (or can attach) to. One of these, to be sure, is the narrative itself. There is such a thing as liking or disliking the story of a film and distinguishing that reaction from one's reaction to its other qualities. Pleasure and/or displeasure may also attach to the social setting of the viewing experience (theater, drive-in, living room, etc.). Obviously this is true of other experiences; that is, one can experience pleasure or displeasure in a social setting whether film is involved or not. But in the regime of film, there is an *expectation* of this kind of pleasure. "Going to the movies" has always held a specific promise and a particular allure—indeed, when I ask students nowadays why they think the VCR has not put all movie theaters out of business, they refer immediately to the movie theater itself and to the act of attending a movie as a social act not adequately substituted for by viewing a film on videotape.

Pleasure and/or displeasure also go beyond the narrative itself, and beyond the social setting, to what we might provisionally term the phenomenon of *spectacle*, meaning those aspects of the film that do not admit of convincing verbal renarration but nonetheless do provide the very pleasure (or displeasure) that separates the film from a verbal renarration. These might include the appearance of the actors; the settings; the music; the cinematography; the presence or absence of violence; the sexual explicitness of the film; and so forth. These things do not, as several generations of film theorists have shown us, operate completely outside of "the story." The experience of a narrative film *includes* spectacle and pleasurable or displeasurable reactions to aspects of it. But what I am calling "spectacle" is distinct from narrative, not in the sense that it is not part of the film, but in the sense that it is not part of the narrative that the film tells and that we, as viewers of the film, often have occasion to tell again.

Pleasure is thus in some sense the analog, in film, to power in law. This is not to say that they are the same; rather, it is to suggest that both of these regimes revolve committedly around narrative but purvey something else at the same time. Indeed, filmic pleasure is not contingent on any particular type of narrative nor, arguably, on narrative coherence itself; one may take great pleasure in surrealist films, for instance, without feeling that one can retell the "story" accurately. Pornography provides perhaps the limiting case. Pornographic films are certainly narrative, and many or most are narratives in the sense of having a cohesive story line. At the same time, the pleasure of pornography generally lies outside of the narrative trajectory per se.

Like legal power, then, filmic pleasure does not entirely depend on narrative—it can be exercised more or less outside of narrativity—but it does, as an empirical matter, tend to be made available through narrative in the vast majority of cases. (I will pursue later the question of *why* this is the case.) Moreover, and also like legal power, filmic pleasure is discriminatory—which might mean any of several things. It certainly might mean that some of the pleasure taken in film stems from discriminatory politics—that is, from the consequences of the fact that commercial film has appointed itself as a kind of time capsule for the preservation of racial and gender stereotypes.[9] The statement that filmic pleasure is discriminatory might also refer to the fact that the invitation to pleasure is extended to different people in the cases of different films. This is a matter of marketing: there are children's films, adult suspense films, art films, and so forth. Another way to frame this—or to invert it into a more reception-aware formulation—is to say that different people take different kinds and amounts of pleasure in different films and, indeed, that they do so whether they are the people directly targeted for such pleasure by the film industry or not. After all, pleasure taken is not always identical to pleasure offered; there are plenty of adults, for instance, who take possibly guilty pleasure in children's films (it makes a big difference to many parents whether their child is going through the *Mary Poppins* phase [good] or *The Little Mermaid* phase [bad]). If any mismatches between targeted audiences and actual fandom qualifies as misbehavior on the part of pleasure, such misbehavior is nonetheless part of the regime; at least, it does not adversely affect the ultimate goal of the regime—economic profit—which in the end is not contingent on the age or predicted tastes of viewers.

If filmic pleasure is discriminatory at both the production and consumption ends, its discriminatory procedures are nonetheless hardly as weighty as those of law. But the differences and similarities are instructive. It is the function of law to conceal its discrimination; the legal system is a discriminatory regime that tries to present itself as a fair one. Film, on the other hand, is a very fair regime—one whose narratives and pleasures are easily to hand—that packages itself as discriminatory. Films are marketed and "imaged" for particular consumers. The regime of film includes an endless, industrious process of public, private, written, spoken, and demographic discrimination—and, unlike law, it keeps this process very much on the surface.

Nowhere is this productivity of discriminatory discourse more evident than in the subregime of published film criticism, the clear purpose of which is to discriminate among films, both on narrative grounds and with respect to pleasure (narrative and/or spectacular). That the reactions of critics do not, in fact, have very much to do with anyone's actual pleasure or displeasure in a given film is not the point. Taken at face value—that is, as a mechanism for getting the largest audiences to the "best" films—the review mill is inefficient, if not doomed to meaninglessness. It exists, however, and plays a very key—and very efficient—role in the perpetuation of the discriminatory aspects of the regime of commercial film, as understood here.

Film has in common with law not only the status of narrative regime dependent on discriminatory practices but also a strong tendency toward logomorphism. This assertion (which should be understood in connection with my earlier "position statement" on the matter of narrative and its logomorphic core) may seem counterintuitive: after all, the "point" is supposed to be that film is a metaverbal, experiential, visceral, musical, visual thing. In practical terms, what it means to point to film's logomorphism is to say that there is a tremendous amount of verbal discourse in, about, and around films. The regime of film is saturated with language.[10] Typically, narrative films begin life in verbal form (novel, treatment, screenplay, etc.), enjoy a kind of brief middle life as film, and then, in a sense, revert back to language. What we take with us from a screening of a film is not the film but a logomorph: a mental residuum that, while it exists alongside memories of the visual and aural aspects of the film (the spectacle), permits

us—licenses us, as it were—to retell the film. The memories of pleasure may be unutterable, but the plot is not. To watch a film may be to
travel experientially through time under narrative escort; but it is also
to be consigned a logomorphic—that is, potentially verbalized—impression of the film.

Sure enough, after film emerges from its middle life on the screen, it
finds itself told and retold, synopsized and summarized, in language.
This is the heart of the logomorphism of film: the fact that, in film
culture *as it is*, the majority of viewing experiences leave the viewer
with the necessary credentials to function as renarrator of the film—
and that function is very frequently performed. For all that we talk
about film as a visual medium, the commercial regime of cinema has
in fact gone in for a very word-saturated mode of propagation.

This is, of course, not uniquely true of film; we might say virtually
the same thing of experience itself (i.e., that we verbalize and summarize it after we have moved on from its particular time frame). To that
extent, I am trafficking in truisms; but there is more to it, because film
has a *choice*. Film can opt—or perhaps one should say, could have
opted—for a far greater ineffability than it normally does. In this sense,
film has as good a shot as any at living up to Pater's dictum that all art
aspires to the condition of music. I will pursue the matter of film's
choosing a narrative/logomorphic gestalt below. For the moment, the
key point is that, like law, film does embrace these principles.

Beyond narrative, in law, lies power; beyond narrative, in film, lies
pleasure. But they also share each other's qualities, after a fashion: film
wields a kind of power, and law provides a certain kind of pleasure.

And in film *about* law, perhaps, lies something of both.

The Choice of Narrative in Film and Law

Film   Christian Metz and others have argued that mainstream commercial film did not have to be predominantly narrative. As Metz puts
it, "The merging of the cinema and of narrativity was a great fact, which
was by no means predestined."[11] He suggests that "there was nothing
unavoidable, or particularly natural, in this [the taking over of the
greater part of total cinematic production by the feature-length narra-
tive]."[12] This is to say that the technology of cinema, as such, did not
lead inexorably to the narrative-based forms we overwhelmingly encounter in the cinema. As I suggested earlier, we do not stroll down to
our corner cinema to watch lengths of leader, or tune in to Siskel and

Ebert disposing their thumbs in judgment upon abstract geometrical films. But, for all that the technology of film has to say about it, we might.

Acceptance of the premise that narrativity and film were not joined at film's birth—and I do accept it—incurs the need to explain the fact of their subsequent conjunction. Narrative, I would suggest in this connection, may be understood as a *choice* on the part of dominant commercial cinema. The use of the term "choice" as a descriptor of film history, in turn, requires clarification, and I shall put the notion into higher relief, first, by briefly indicating other historical developments that might be understood as choices, in the same sense,[13] and second, by suggesting several *reasons* for the particular choice of narrative as organizing principle.

An example of a "choice" made for dominant cinema—not a particularly simple example—is the star system. Masquerading as "giving the audience what it wants," the star system gave the film industry a great deal that *it* wanted: a channel of easy access to mass-distributed publications; a (relative) regularization of what might otherwise have been unmanageable personnel problems; a royal road to the unconscious of the spectator.[14] There was, to paraphrase Metz on narrative, nothing unavoidable, or particularly natural, about the practice of priming and training young performers, developing essentially fictional public personae for them, and holding them out as psychosexual bait to the masses. Rather, this practice, in all its glory, was *chosen* because of the benefits it offered the industry.

Another, somewhat multifaceted example of a "choice" made by commercial cinema is the choice to adopt an agenda of empirically driven realism. This is to say that film has, over time, "added" to itself the properties of sound, color, width of field, sonic directionality, and other items selected from the master shopping list of the phenomenal world. Referring to these developments, collectively, as a "choice" may seem spiteful of realism's apparent logic (after all, sound, color, etc., do exist in the world) or artificially unifying in its packaging together of multiple, historically distinct changes. However, it is important to remember that nothing in the technology "film" necessitated the adoption of this agenda; films were already films when they were silent and in black and white, and they were already able to sustain a profitable industry. What commercial film gained by embarking on the realist odyssey was a supply—probably in perpetuity, since there will always be differences between film and life—of potential innovations that, at critical moments, can serve the important purpose of giving the audience something new to want.

The centrality of narrative to film, I suggest, was a choice at the same logical level as the star system or the realist agenda: not a necessary concomitant of the existence or practice of film, but something brought (heavily) to bear on it for a variety of nonessential—but historically concrete—reasons. I will sketch out three such reasons; two chiefly to illustrate what a "reason to become predominantly narrative" looks like and the third in more direct pursuit of the present argument.

Some evidence of the kind presented by John L. Fell suggests that one of the reasons for the hegemony of narrative in the early cinema was the career continuity of some of its practitioners (D. W. Griffith, with his theatrical background and literary orientation, being a prime example).[15] The idea of crossover between cinema and other narrative practices is familiar enough; it is intriguing to consider it as a "reason" for the choice of narrative. Such an approach would have to distinguish among strands of analogy at the level of the implementation of narrative techniques (Griffith and Dickens, for instance) and junctures where the practitioner's background seemed to determine the choice of narrative forms initially (Griffith and the theater, perhaps, and other similar cases from the previous decade).

Another reason for the choice of narrative as the mode of dominant cinema, formulated by Robert C. Allen, is the production efficiency and degree of control possible in the production of fiction films: "By substituting the fictional events of the comedy picture for the actual events of the topical film, producers regained some of the control over motion picture subject matter they had relinquished in the rush to duplicate the success of the Lumières' 'vues de plein air' in 1896. . . . The scenic and narrative requirements of the comedy film could be made to conform to the limitations of the studio and its environs."[16] Allen does not restrict the observation to comedy: "a hypothesis might be generated to the effect that, in part at least, the need to regain control of the production situation provided the impetus for the development of the dramatic narrative film . . . [which,] like its comic cousin, by creating its own fictional world obviated the need to tie a production to the outside world."[17]

The third and, as promised, particularly salient reason for the choice of narrative as the chief mode of dominant cinema was, I believe, the establishment of its proximity to existing modes of verbal discourse and activity. As narrative, film was advantageously positioned with respect to familiar practices of promotion and dissemination, both by its own efforts and by easy word-of-mouth communication among viewers and potential viewers. By choosing to be narrative—propositional, recountable, logomorphic—the cinema economized enormously on cultural absorption time—indeed, virtually guaranteed its own currency in popular culture. The fact that films are *verbally* available (through paraphrase, synopsis, and description) is anything but a hardship or an irony. In fact, such verbal activity in all its proliferation can be understood not as a compromise with other forms of expression but as a commercial necessity—a cultural practice *in the interest of assuring the perpetuation of which film was decreed narrative.* Film is narrative, in other words (and among other reasons), *so that* we can more easily talk about films.

The conjunction of film and narrative, then, may be described as a choice, inasmuch as (1) there were other possibilities for film not precluded on ontological grounds; (2) the adoption of narrative is logically similar to the adoption of other practices (so that the term "choice" as a descriptor of film history gains some substance by its applicability beyond this one case); and (3) reasons can be adduced for the choice, consisting largely of commercial benefits accruing to the film industry as it branched away from *non*narrative practices. While there was more to this choice than its easy or spontaneous selection from an array of other, equally available choices, its designation as precisely a "choice" takes us away from the perspective that the narrative cinema as we know it was a necessary consequence of film technology—and away from the easily associated notion that narrativity is an inalienable or irreducible aspect of filmic representation.

Law   The centrality of narrative to legal procedure also represents a choice; and the recognition of this condition meets as much resistance as its counterpart in the case of film. Bennett and Feldman put storytelling in perspective—not by denouncing it outright, but by being very clear about its function relative to the system it supports, and by discussing both forms of judicial administration other than the jury trial and the "implicit judgment practices" that function within those other forms as storytelling does in our system:

There are various forms of adjudication, and each form involves different implicit judgment practices and displays a different notion of how to do justice. One form is oath taking; another is trial by ordeal; another is trial by jury or judge. There are undoubtedly other forms. . . . [The] achievement of justice is not so much dependent on the procedure, per se, as on the societal acceptance of the procedure and the coherence of societal beliefs with the procedure.[18]

There follows a discussion of several examples of alternate means of achieving justice, the most striking of which is perhaps the report of John C. Messenger Jr.'s work on the Anang adjudication process, which involves in part the attempts of the plaintiff and defendant to produce proverbs that best summarize their respective positions. Bennett and Feldman explain the function of the proverb in the process, where it is analogous to the use of well-crafted stories in the American courts:

Objective legal judgment in Anang does not exist in some metaphysical world apart from the actual legal procedures employed in Anang courts. Objective legal judgment is defined by the search for the proverb that best captures the issues and evidence in a case. Since proverbs are, by definition, the most universally accepted statements of normative propositions among the Anang, the proverb that provides the best fit for a case also introduces an established and enduring principle of judgment appropriate for the legal resolution of the case.[19]

Bennett and Feldman's isolation of the implicit judgment practices in a given legal system enables them to put storytelling in perspective as something chosen for various reasons, filling a position in the system that can be and is filled by other practices at other times and in other societies.

Thus, to the extent that film and law share a commitment to narrative as organizing principle, they share too the historical fact of having chosen narrative for that role—a choice made for identifiable and nonrandom reasons, but a choice, rather than a necessity, nonetheless. There is room already for a number of questions that I will not pursue at any length here. We might ask, for instance, whether any narrative-based cultural practice can be said *not* to have "chosen" narrative. (News comes to mind. If news were nonnarrative, would it still be news, as film is still film and legal procedure is still legal procedure?) In the interests of rhetorical pace, however, I shall move on to further parallels that, each in its own way, lie in the general orbit of the parallel of narrative activity.

The Denial of Language

Dominant American cinema and dominant American trial procedure have both "chosen" narrative as their basis. Still, for all their mutual dedication to narrative, there seems somehow to be a different significance to *saying* that film takes the telling of stories as its main aim and *saying* the same thing about law. Describing the commercial cinema as a story factory has the ring of compliance with its face-value claims, while making the same characterization of the legal system, even in the broadest terms, sounds distinctly critical and skeptical. What is the significance of this difference?

The observation of the difference noted here represents, I believe, not a flaw in the theory that the two institutions peddle narrative in similar ways but a revelation of certain differences in their respective compositions. That is, what turns out to be different is not the basic principle at work but the economies of power and representation in the two regimes.

This difference can be clarified if we tease apart, in each case, the institution's ostensible function from its master purpose. In the case of film, the ostensible function is to provide entertainment; its master purpose is to make money. The ostensible function of the legal system is to administer justice; its master purpose, to put it somewhat broadly, is to keep existing power structures in place and postpone the final stages of social chaos. Both institutions generate narrative. The cinema, however, can safely advertise and celebrate its commitment to narrative—and has reason to do so. It has an institutional need to publicize its own properties in terms other than those of its master purpose; and its ostensible function happens to be one that can coexist peacefully with an emphasis on narrative.

Though similarly motivated, the law is fitted out with a different configuration of terms. The judicial system needs to do what the cinema needs to do—draw attention away from its master purpose—and it does so by advertising its ostensible function, as cinema does. However, as it turns to its ostensible function to provide a decoy from its master purpose, its committedness to the production of narratives must go unconfessed, because that committedness cannot easily be reconciled with the claim that the effect of legal process is the administration of justice. The law shares cinema's basis in the generation of narrative. But, whereas the generation of narrative is compatible with the ostensible function of cinema, it is not compatible with the ostensible function of the law. (As for the judicial system's choice of ostensible purpose—perhaps entertainment would have meshed better with narrative, but the handing down of justice has a loftier, historically somewhat more prestigious image.)

In a related way, the two institutions' internal economies also differ with respect to the relations therein among narrativity, narration, and veristic referentiality. Film has the task of making a sensory and referential miscellany into narrative, available for effortless synopsis and dissemination. The law, on the other hand, has materially available to it, almost exclusively, finished verbal narrative; it must therefore devote its energy to enhancing the apparent leverage of that verbal narrative over an *absent* miscellany of events and referents. Thus, the two regimes operate in inverse or complementary ways: in the case of film, narrativity depends on the concealment of the miscellaneous, syncretic properties of the text; while in legal process, the narrative's task is to convey the assurance that an irrevocably lost miscellany is, in fact, present.

Both of these agendas constitute, after a fashion, a denial of language. Narrative film plays up its own immediacy, the presence in the projection of the represented past. It does not flaunt the fact that, as a narrative regime, it largely confines itself to that which can be cognitively funneled into language—indeed, into the fairly specialized narrative form "story." In other words, film celebrates the *difference* between itself and language, between the imaged event and its subsequent verbal reconstruction, despite its institutional mandate to keep that difference to a minimum. Legal process, on the other hand, argues the *identity* of the heterogenous world of past events and the language that represents that world, particularly in court. It, too, thus denies language—that is, it denies the difference between past events and the language in which they are symbolically reconstructed. Verbal discourse must be trusted as a stand-in for events; the regime depends, in effect, on no one's being too disturbed by the fact that it is language, not events, on view.

Thus, the two institutions, in complementary ways, deny language. In the cinema, whose attraction lies in the impression of the presence of actual events, the centrality of the verbal is a liability. The greatest liability of legal process, however, is the irretrievability of actual events; and the response is a cultivation of faith in the adequacy of language as surrogate for the past.

Notes

1. W. Lance Bennett and Martha S. Feldman, *Reconstructing Reality in the Courtroom: Justice and Judgment in American Culture* (New Brunswick, N.J.: Rutgers University Press, 1981), 8. I am allowing a certain slippage here between the notions of "narrative" and "storytelling." Bennett and Feldman organize their argument around the latter term; taken from their structuralist perspective, "story" corresponds closely to at least one form of what I have called "*a* narrative."

2. The horse—that is, a more extensive account of the law-as-literature movement—occurs in chapter 6. For the present purpose, it suffices to note that the law-as-literature movement has tended to posit what amounts to a relationship of equality (rather than one of analogy) between legal processes and literary and/or literary-theoretical, interpretive activities.

3. Robin West, "Adjudication Is Not Interpretation: Some Reservations about the Law-as-Literature Movement," *Tennessee Law Review* 54 (Fall 1986): 207. Interestingly, West's article is a "law-in-literature" essay (she is one of the movement's central figures as well as a critic of certain aspects of it) In it she explores contemporary legal theory through the prism of Twain's *Pudd'nhead Wilson* and John Barth's novel *The Floating Opera.*

4. Crime may of course involve texts and textuality (as in the case of libel law); but crime itself is not in the first instance a textual phenomenon.

5. I report this from distant television memory. The food in question, I believe, was ants or water or some combination of those two staples.

6. This is not to say that abstract geometrical shapes cannot be narrativized—indeed, such narrativization of the nonnarrative probably lies at the root of all narrative cognition.

7. I do not remember which issue of *TV Guide* this synopsis appeared in. Of possible interest, however (at least to those among my readers who believe that I have not made the example up), is the fact that other issues of the magazine had somewhat longer synopses, of which this brief sentence was a part. In other words, the extremity of the example seems to owe itself to the vagaries of page layout.

8. Moreover, we might actually experience pleasure at the revelation of a chance to see the film.

9. Later I will pursue aspects of this possibility in connection with the matter of plausibility in film and law.

10. I must reemphasize that I am not making a case for a theory of filmic cognition based in linguistic analogy (although such theories are extremely

interesting and have loomed very large). Rather, I am making the more mundane but for present purposes more urgent point that people talk about, paraphrase, summarize, and synopsize films verbally—at home, on the phone, at work, all the time.

11. Christian Metz, *Film Language: A Semiotics of the Cinema*, trans. Michael Taylor (New York: Oxford University Press, 1967), 93.

12. Ibid., 44.

13. Of course, *any* choice made by the film industry may be subsumed into the black hole represented by profit making—the first and last "choice." By refracting the profit motive into some of its spectral components, one is in a sense pulling against the tide, but doing so in the hope of pointing out something informative or revealing—as one might opt to discuss a baseball season in more detailed terms than simply uttering the name of the team that won the World Series.

14. I will not take up here at any length the vexed issue of whether the film industry (along with other media) does indeed "give the audience what it wants." For what it's worth, I tend to believe that the film industry tells the audience to want the various things that it, the industry, has decided to provide.

15. See John L. Fell, *Film and the Narrative Tradition* (1974; rpt., Berkeley: University of California Press, 1986).

16. Robert C. Allen, *Vaudeville and Film, 1895–1915: A Study in Media Interaction* (New York: Arno Press, 1980), 157.

17. Ibid., 158.

18. Bennett and Feldman, 22.

19. Ibid., 29. Bennett and Feldman refer their readers to John C. Messenger Jr., "The Role of Proverbs in a Nigerian Judicial System," *Southwestern Journal of Anthropology* 15 (1959): 64–73.

Part 2

Knowing Law in Film

3

Genre and Its Alternatives

A Syllogistic Starting Point: Automatic Reflexivity

It's time for an encounter between law and film—time to parlay the basic observation of their shared grounding in narrative as organizing principle into a theoretical apparatus capable of saying something about their conjunction. To summarize the underlying premises:

1. The products of the commercial cinema, for the most part and indeed almost exclusively, are narrative fiction films; that is, they tell stories.
2. The legal processes we are concerned with also, in their own way, revolve around processes of narration and storytelling: legal investigators piece together stories; witnesses tell stories; legal advocates tell and retell stories; and judges and juries evaluate stories on criteria of plausibility and narrative coherence.

Making another pass, we can fold these premises into a syllogism:

A. Legal processes, to a large degree, involve or revolve around processes of narration and storytelling.
B. Films about law are (like other films) narratives or instances of storytelling.
C. Therefore, films about law are stories about the process of storytelling, or *narratives about narrative.*

Stories about storytelling, or narratives about narrative, have been characterized in the field of textual criticism as self-reflexive or, to use the shorter term I will favor here, *reflexive.* Reflexivity will serve us centrally as a common and connecting property of films about law, a theoretical "home base" from which other ways of looking at films-about-law may be examined and evaluated, and a major principle of organization and analysis.

The roots of the notion of reflexivity lie in grammar: a reflexive verb is one whose subject and indirect object are the same. A working definition of reflexivity in the sphere of literary and other creative texts might take its cue from this: a reflexive text is a text that, in one or more ways, takes itself as the object of its own representation.

In fact, reflexivity in textual theory is an exponentially more complex matter than reflexivity in grammar (though not necessarily a more profound one). The claim that a text—book, film, television show, and so forth—takes itself as its own object raises the rather nontrivial question of what exactly the "self" of a text is. In the case of film, the "self" represented by a reflexive text may have to do with any or all of several registers of the text's structure, content, and history. In *Reflexivity in Film and Literature* (the locus classicus of the study of reflexivity in film), Robert Stam addresses several of these registers, which are reflected in aspects of the organization of his book.[1] His first chapter, "Allegories of Spectatorship," explores the various ways in which the conditions and processes of cinematic spectatorship can find a place on the thematic and representational agenda of films. Here, already, there is considerable sweep to the topic. To begin with, a film may explicitly examine the processes of spectatorship. Stam's examples in this regard go back to Porter's *Uncle Josh at the Moving Picture Show*, "which initiates a venerable tradition in which the humor derives from a hayseed's naiveté in his first encounter with the filmic medium."[2] Uncle Josh (a recurrent figure in Edison films and phonograph records around the turn of the century) goes to the movies and mistakes representation for real life. While we presumably do not accede quite to his level of gullibility, he nonetheless is "our [double] insofar as [his] naive faith in spectacle resembles our own spectatorial investment in illusionistic fictions."[3]

A film may also take cinematic spectatorship as the object of representation in less-concrete, less-literal ways. Stam explores this path in an extended treatment of Hitchcock's *Rear Window*, a film that does not include a single shot of a theater, projector, or screen but that constitutes, nonetheless, a "brilliant filmic essay on the cinema and on the nature of the cinematic experience."[4] The reflexivity of such a film may be grasped by means of abstraction, analogy, or even syllogism: *Rear Window* is about what watching a movie is about—which is to say, at least in large part, voyeurism. This syllogistic premise, however, does not make for a "less" reflexive or less powerfully reflexive film. As Stam's treatment of the matter clearly demonstrates, *Rear Window* offers a far more sustained and penetrating essay on the nature of filmic spectatorship than does the more literally cinema-centered *Uncle Josh.*

Reflexivity in film, then, may pertain to spectatorship; that is, spectatorship is part of the "self" that, under the present working definition, reflexive films are about. Stam's second chapter, "The Process of Production," deals with a second key area of filmic reflexivity. By convention, narrative films do everything they can to disguise not only the details but the very fact of their production or produced-ness; when we speak of illusionism in filmic representation—or, for that matter, of realism—we speak primarily of a large range of photographic, dramatic, and editorial practices that, taken together (and in association with culturally conditioned cognitive processing), encourage and enable us to forget that what we are seeing is mediated, artificial, and irreducibly unreal. In this connection, Stam examines a number of films that "take as their subject either the cinematic institution or the concrete technical or aesthetic operations involved in filmmaking." This algorithm of selection leads Stam to a consideration of such films as Wilder's *Sunset Boulevard* (a film that "explores the superimposed crises—economic, technological, esthetic—besetting Hollywood" in the postwar era[5]); Fellini's *8½* and Truffaut's *Day for Night* (both films about the process of making films); and Fassbinder's *Veronika Voss* (the story of a faded film star).

As indicated, the claim that films about law are reflexive stems from syllogistic or triangular reasoning: such films are, at once, *narratives* and *about law,* while at the same time law is "about" (i.e., organized around, saturated in) narrative. No component of this cluster of practices is completely unique to the cluster. Law and cinema are not our only narrative institutions. Nor must a film represent legal processes in order to exhibit reflexivity—indeed, even to exhibit the "story-about-storytelling" strain of reflexivity. *Frankenstein,* to choose only one example, depicts a group of people telling each other stories and therefore may claim the same status. The singular nature of the reflexivity of films about law stems not from one thing or the other but from their convergence in one place. The very professions of law are professions of story reconstruction, comprehension, and telling. Therefore, any reference to the legal profession harbors a reference to storytelling. The nonlegal example of *Frankenstein* demonstrates that any character in a film can be shown telling a story; but the mere presence of those people, or a reference to their professional milieus, would not in and of itself evoke the kinds of elaborate and ritualized acts of story construction and telling around which law is built.

We all tell stories (with or without a thunderstorm, à la *Frankenstein*, as a pretext). But only a few people narrate, or construct narrative, for a living. Legal investigators and advocates do, and so do filmmakers. Thus, *films about* legal investigation and advocacy may be understood as cousins of *films about* the underlying processes of film. The same kind of relation may be traced in the realm of physical spaces. Narrative springs up everywhere. But only a few social or institutional spaces exist *for the purpose* of allowing people to assemble and to tell, hear, and (dis)believe a series of ritually constructed, conventionally verisimilar narratives. The courtroom is one such place; the movie theater is another; and their superimposition—that is, the filling of one by a representation of the other—has a privileged status among configurations of fictional subject matter and medium.

Although I will troubleshoot and refine it, the initial theoretical claim I am making for films-about-law is a broad and inclusive one: namely, that the *very presence* of the representation of legal processes in a film automatically betokens reflexivity—or, to put it another way, all films that include representation of legal process may be said to possess an *automatic reflexivity.*

This claim clearly operates at an enormously general level; it amounts to an axiom. Anything one says about every film in which there is law *must* be a vast generality. Indeed, automatic reflexivity is only the beginning; the sweep of the claim should be understood not as a conclusion or summation but as the flicking of a switch, the introduction of a current—a theoretical charge—running at least measurably through every film in which law appears and capable, not in every case but in many, of tremendous gain.

Reflexivity and/or Genre

Genre is the traditional and perhaps more intuitive approach to doing what the automatic reflexivity axiom does: namely, identifying a body of films and investigating the common positioning of certain themes within those films and of the films themselves in a broader cultural context. Ultimately, I see the approach rooted in the axiom of automatic reflexivity as an alternative theoretical framework, one that both logically precedes and critically complements genre analysis, and I will develop it in that light. The guiding principle in the current study is automatic reflexivity, not genre; but the points of contact, and instructive contrasts, are important and numerous enough that a further reckoning with the idea of genre is in order. For that reason alone, the relation between genre and automatic reflexivity, as critical frameworks, deserves a full accounting. To be sure, the films brought together by the automatic reflexivity axiom do not constitute a genre. The axiom is clearly *too* inclusive for that to be the case. Accordingly, the purpose of what follows here is not to determine whether we are dealing with a generic corpus (which we are definitely not) but to bring the automatic reflexivity approach into higher relief through a comparison, sustained into a medium level of detail, with its most important neighboring and antecedent methodology.

To begin with, part of the complexity of the critical approach based in reflexivity stems from the fact that films about law do in fact fall into genres—that is, in respect of the whole matter of grouping and subgrouping films about law, the slate is not clean and reflexivity is neither the first nor only way to do it. The clearest case for a law-in-film genre can probably be made for the existence of a courtroom genre, to which, inter alia, *Inherit the Wind, Anatomy of a Murder, I Confess,* and *To Kill a Mockingbird* would belong. The courtroom genre itself, moreover, arguably contains subgenres, clustering around various and distinctive focal topics such as jurors (*Twelve Angry Men, The Juror*), military courts (*A Few Good Men, Breaker Morant*), or even nonliteral courtrooms (*M, The Ox-Bow Incident*). In addition to these provisional mappings of a composite courtroom genre, we might successfully take a genre-theoretical approach to films revolving around the depiction of prisons (which might even turn out to be a subgenre of "legal punishment" films) or police and detective work. In short, films-about-law offer the genre theorist as many opportunities and challenges as any other broad category of film—Westerns, comedies, and so forth.

Some of the thematic divisions listed above have provided the basis for published anthologies of film descriptions and analyses, though such publications do not necessarily include a thorough reckoning with the theoretical nuances of genre analysis. Indeed, such a reckoning would be a major task or, more accurately, a succession of major tasks. The results would probably be interesting and worthwhile; however, the body of films brought together under the banner of automatic reflexivity—that is, all films that contain *any* amount of representation of *any* legal process—is both larger and more intractable, from the point of view of genre theory, than the sum of all the films that might qualify as members of one or the other legal genre. In other words, the axiom of automatic reflexivity gives us a superset of any imaginable legal genre, subgenre, or even supergenre.

Quality Time: The Matter of On-screen Duration   It is not necessary to repudiate the notion of genre in order to pursue an inquiry organized around reflexivity. The two approaches can coexist. At the same time, it seems to me that the reflexivity approach has a certain logical priority. As a general matter, legal process in film does not behave like a genre. It is too available—a condiment rather than an entrée. Any film can (and many do) include a cursory courtroom scene, a perfunctory arrest, or a few shots inside a prison. Thus, by the broad criteria suggested here, any film can easily "become" a film-about-law at any point, courtesy of a shot or two. A film cannot, however, become a musical, a Western, a horror film, or a screwball comedy for a few seconds here and there (unless in lampoon or parody), but legal process is always an option, always at the ready. Furthermore, the significance of the representation of law is not always a matter of length or even centrality of that representation. We need an approach that can treat the representation of legal processes in fiction film wherever and for however long it appears and however demonstrative of genre membership it may or may not be.[6]

Automatic reflexivity, in other words, neither depends on nor varies with the duration of the representation of legal themes in a given film. This does not mean that one automatically reflexive film cannot differ from another in a vast number of important ways, including ways that pertain directly to reflexivity in a more expansive (nonautomatic) sense. It also does not mean that duration never matters. Duration can indicate, at least roughly, membership of film in a genre—for example, when forty minutes of a film are set in a courtroom and the trial participants are the film's main characters. Ultimately, genre too deserves a more nuanced definition than one rooted in screen time. But the main point here is to make a distinction—preliminary, but decisive—between the entire matter of genre (of which, in the case of the representation of law, screen duration may serve as a rough index) and the entire matter of automatic reflexivity (of which screen duration, though not necessarily irrelevant to *all* manifestations of reflexivity, is not an index).

Inversely, even the nonuse of duration as a criterion of inclusion—that is, the constitution of a generic body that includes at least some films with very short scenes about law—does not guarantee that reflexivity has been taken into account. From the point of view of theory and criticism, automatic reflexivity begins life as an axiom or even an assertion; but for it to be taken beyond that point, actual effort is required. *That* part of reflexivity does not happen automatically, and any approach to studying films about law that does not address it directly has not unearthed it fully.

Synthesizing these observations, we can note examples of the consequences of *sidestepping reflexivity to get to genre* in the study of films about law. One example is Paul Bergman and Michael Asimow's *Reel Justice: The Courtroom Goes to the Movies.*[7] Admittedly, this book is more a de facto genre study than an explicit one; but it does illustrate, if only symptomatically, both the interest for critics of the automatic reflexivity of films about law (courtroom films, in this case) and the costs of leaving that reflexivity unexplored.

In his foreword to the book, Judge Alex Kozinski suggests that "the moviemaker's art is not all that different from the lawyer's—especially the courtroom advocate's. Both must capture, in a very short space, a slice of human existence, and make the audience see a story from their particular perspective. Both have to know which facts to include and which ones to leave out; when to appeal to emotion and when to reason; . . . when to script and when to improvise."[8]

These parallels are accurate, and they point to at least one area of automatic reflexivity (or even the underpinnings of automatic reflexivity): an important resemblance arising from institutional convergences between law and film, lying outside any particular film or law-in-film genre. The book, however, does not monopolize on the insights in the foreword. Rather, it moves in what might even be described as the opposite direction: away from the level of rhetorical underpinning and toward a legally informed but theoretically uninquisitive realism. Each of the sixty-nine films discussed receives its own section, including a "legal analysis" that evaluates the film's handling of legal process for plausibility and accuracy. Along the way a great deal of interesting information about legal technicalities emerges. But the crudity of the "would-this-really-happen?" approach to narrative criticism takes its toll and cuts off at the pass any insightful treatment of the entanglement of legal and filmic cultural idioms. ("Thus," the authors write, "*Bananas* screws up both legal rules and trial procedures. Real cases are nothing like this. Too bad."[9])

The Courtroom Film: A Provisional Generic Approach

Rick Altman and the Theory of Genre   *Reel Justice* does not claim to be a theoretical treatise on either genre or reflexivity; its relevance here lies in its symptomatic behavior, which illustrates at least broadly the nonnecessity of making connections between genre and automatic reflexivity (even where there seems to be an opening to do so). In pursuit of a further level of detail in the matter of the relation between automatic reflexivity and genre, I turn next to a book that has the opposite status: it *is* a theoretical treatise on genre but does not have to do with films about law. That book is Rick Altman's *American Film Musical.*[10] I will engage Altman's genre-theoretical ideas in the services of an attempt—experimental and limited in its relevance to the present project—to think through what would be involved in establishing a meaningful courtroom genre. The focus on the courtroom introduces a certain asymmetry, since our starting point in exploring automatic reflexivity is the totality of films about various types of legal process. But the one step of narrowing the field, temporarily, to courtroom film allows for interaction between Altman's approach and mine that might otherwise not occur.

Altman describes *The American Film Musical* as "not one book, but two."

> Most overtly, it is an account of the Hollywood musical and its place in American life. . . .
>
> But what is the musical? How do we define it, delimit it, and analyze it? . . . More than any other realm in the general domain of film studies, genre criticism has remained complacently untheoretical, accepting terms and categories provided by an openly self-serving industry, borrowing notions of history from fan magazines, and overall revealing shockingly little methodological self-consciousness.
>
> In response to this situation, I have felt compelled to make this book into something more than the story of a genre. From beginning to end, *The American Film Musical* is also a treatise on how to study genre.[11]

The musical thus serves as a sustained case study for the establishment of a rigorous and systematic approach to the study of genre overall. Altman explicitly voices the hope that the theoretical and methodological framework he develops might find application in the work of other theorists of other genres.[12]

One of Altman's major concerns, both in connection with the musical and throughout the "genre theory" trajectory of the book, is the matter of identifying the corpus of films that constitute the genre, a process he feels has suffered in the past from lack of rigor and a failure on the part of genre critics to come to terms with their own historical positioning. Altman explores several principles of genre study that, in various ways, bear directly on the matter of selecting and defining a generic corpus. In the first instance, he suggests, the genre theorist should cast a wide net, catching a large number of films and roughing out a relatively indiscriminate corpus that subsequently will be reduced and clarified according to more refined criteria of inclusion. Hollywood and the press, for example, already use the term "musical" and already mean something by it. The films—all the films—to which that term attaches, as indexed by industrial and journalistic usage, belong in the large, unrefined corpus.

But the genre critic's work only begins where the rough aggregation of "musicals," in this very broad sense, ends. The very inclusive meaning, Altman argues, serves the needs of producers (for whom a category like "musical" relates directly to concerns of planning and budgeting) and consumers (who can safely make certain aesthetic assumptions about any film that Hollywood calls a "musical"). For critics, however,

> the industrial definition of the genre is of extremely limited interest. . . . Far from seeking to explain the genre or its texts, far from creating a vocabulary appropriate both to systematic and historical analysis, Hollywood's version of the musical serves only to locate the genre, rather than to provide a method of dealing with its functioning or even of justifying this particular delimitation of the genre. Just as the medieval fisherman called everything that swims in the water a fish, so Hollywood calls everything that shows music on film a musical. . . . Does the musical have its whales? Are there texts commonly called musicals which in fact operate according to a logic different from the vast majority of other musicals?[13]

The problem with the familiar, received notions about musicals, for Altman, is that those notions neither are, nor ever were, developed by genre critics, yet they have always been *mistaken* for genre-critical categories. The broadly inclusive corpus is flawed for being too easy to deal with, too intuitive, too easily pressed into service as the meaningful generic body that ultimately it cannot claim to be. Altman thus advocates filtering a relatively raw system of definitions (though not a meaningless one) through a more refined and critically accountable process. He proposes neither an arbitrary narrowing process nor a wholesale refusal of Hollywood's understanding of the term but a thorough renegotiation of the corpus that the term has traditionally indicated—using that traditional, very inclusive corpus as a starting point:

> The broadest possible corpus implied by the industrial/journalistic term is taken as the critic's *preliminary* corpus. In the case of the musical, this means that every conceivable film with diegetic music is at first accepted and treated as a musical. . . .
> . . . The broad amorphous corpus thus borrowed is then subjected to diverse modes of analysis.[14]

As his attention increasingly zeros in on the particular case of the musical, Altman develops and tests such "modes of analysis" and criteria of inclusion, bringing them to bear on the broadly defined "musical" in the interest of establishing a smaller, more rigorously defined generic corpus.

Courtroom and Genre   As a starting point, the formula of inclusion represented by a theory of automatic reflexivity in the case of films about law shares with Altman's "first cut" the quality of inclusiveness. But in the face of an attempt to refine or narrow it, the law-in-film corpus has somewhat the opposite problem from that of the every-conceivable-musical corpus: the corpus consisting of every film that represents law is not an amorphous or undisciplined one but no corpus at all. It exhibits not even the rough outline of a genre. Nor does it invite the kind of transformation into genre theory proposed by Altman in the case of pretheoretical genre inclusiveness. The body of films delineated by the formula "all films that represent law" does not clearly point to a second, subsequent corpus or any way to get to one.

There is more to this, however, than the conclusion that idea cut and pasted from Altman does not universally "work." In fact, I propose, up to a point, to *make* it work; that is, to push the analysis of the huge law-in-film corpus deliberately in the direction of genre analysis in order to bring to the surface as many of the similarities and differences between genre theory and the algorithm of automatic reflexivity as possible. At most, this will result in genre analysis at only a medium level of detail—by design, enough to serve as a kind of placeholder for that approach, for the sake of giving contour to the ongoing treatment of automatic reflexivity.

Put another way, what follows here is an experiment in operating under a genre-theory compulsion; that is, according to the principle that, faced with a mass of films, *finding a genre is always preferable to not finding a genre.* To do this, we need to bridge the gap between the too-sprawling mass of all films about law and a body of films that admits of this treatment while not cutting us adrift from the goal of further, nongeneric analysis. Hence—as indicated above, and in the interest of making the experiment possible while keeping it meaningful—the following experiment in the development of a genre framework will revolve around courtroom films.

Toward the beginning of *The American Film Musical,* Altman maps out his approach to the study of a given genre, in a series of steps paraphrased here:

1. *Found the hypothesis that there is such a genre.* In the case of courtroom films, this might be based on publicity, on use of the phrase "courtroom film" in journalistic criticism, and even on the very existence of books such as *Reel Justice.*

2. *Establish the preliminary (very inclusive) corpus.* It would be possible to use the films covered by *Reel Justice* as a preliminary corpus, although the authors of that book, while not following Altman's approach nor striving for a genre-theoretical position, have clearly already made a lot of choices and selected among numerous available films. On the other hand, the film industry, while aware of the possibility of marketing courtroom films as courtroom films, has not made as major a point of it as with the musical—which means that publicity alone would be difficult to use as a source for the preliminary corpus.[15] Another way to define the preliminary corpus would be as itself a reduction of the all-films-about-law category: in short, *all films that depict, specifically and explicitly, events taking place in a courtroom.* This formula yields a smaller set of films than does the universal law-in-film principle (though not a small one). While that set of films is arrived at through a mechanism somewhat different from the one proposed by Altman for the musical, it shares with the preliminary musical corpus

the quality of requiring further refinement in order to serve as a starting point for real genre-theoretical inquiry.

3. *Subject the preliminary, inclusive corpus to diverse modes of analysis.* Here I will introduce some central problems involved in this stage of defining the courtroom genre and will select provisional solutions.

a. *Duration.* We might consider making an in-or-out distinction between films that include a brief courtroom scene and those that linger in the courtroom. Inevitably, however, this would have to be expressed as a percentage of screen time—which, in its brittleness as a critical measurement, suggests that duration might better be folded into other criteria, such as those bearing on dramaturgy and character placement in narrative space. A courtroom setting might serve as a narrative hub from which various flashbacks and stories emerge, even if the courtroom itself does not remain on-screen for more than a few minutes. There may nonetheless be reason to establish an absolute durational minimum, but such a specification should take into account the relation of screen time to other salient elements.

b. *Literal versus functional courtroom.* A generic reckoning with the courtroom film would have to resolve the question of whether the depiction of an actual courtroom was required or whether other social spaces that were nonetheless functioning as courtrooms might qualify. Classic instances of such functional courtrooms include the thieves' den in *M* and the outdoor space of *The Ox-Bow Incident.* One way around this issue would be the redefinition of the genre as the *trial* genre rather than the courtroom genre; the genre critic could then specify required procedural or dramaturgical elements as criteria of generic inclusion. However, such a modification would somewhat arbitrarily rank procedure above space, in a case where the attributes of the space—in particular, its status as a place where official or governmental legal personnel hold sway—have a lot to do with the significance of the films in the first place.

c. *Formal aspects of the courtroom ritual.* One way to include nonliteral courtrooms would be to define trial procedure by its technical or ritualistic elements. These might include characterological requirements—that is, some determination of the minimum "cast" required for a trial (defendant, judge, prosecutor, etc.); the requirement that all those roles be filled; and various positive assertions about their relations and intentions toward each other. Trial procedure might also be partially defined by the disposition of the participants in space. Trial space itself is usually nonrandom, though not always (cf. *The Ox-Bow Incident*); but even when trial space *is* random, the physical relations among the participants, once established, are not arbitrary. A partial definition of the filmic trial might rest on such spatial-relational criteria.

d. *Narratological criteria.* One imaginable criterion of this kind would be the stipulation that the trial scene may not be the first thing in *plot time*, though it may be the first thing in *screen time.* This would mean, for example, the elimination of *Notorious* from the genre, because the courtroom scene in that film is the earliest story event depicted in the film. The rationale for distinguishing between plot time and screen time is the assumption that a filmic courtroom can only be important enough to qualify the film for designation as a courtroom film if something leads up to it—even if the events leading up to it are represented in flashback. The distinction would allow for the inclusion of films that open in the courtroom but flash back in time at some later point. The plot time/screen time distinction thus bears on the question of the suitability of duration as a criterion of inclusion.

4. *Define the new, smaller corpus.* I will not do this at any length but will let the preceding comments on the merits of various criteria (and the comments evaluating the likelihood of inclusion of various films) suffice.

5. *Deal with the question of genre history.* (I will have more to say about this in chapter 4.) In the large, Altman's work amounts to a fusing of genre theory and genre history. Any genre(s) of films about law we might define could presumably be discussed in the context of genre history. But automatic reflexivity has a different relation to history, one that, while not completely separable from genre history (which might *at times* be relevant to it), has a significantly different shape. Specifically, while any given study of a *particular* genre need not address the question of where *genre itself* came from (though the genre theorist should be informed in this area), the study of automatic reflexivity must—among other things—do precisely that, in its own realm: it must concern itself with its own earliest origins, which are never very far away. Automatic reflexivity comes from history. Films about law can be said to be automatically reflexive *because* filmic practice and legal procedure are both "about" the same historically locatable thing—namely, narrative.

Pursued with tenacity, this Altman-inspired approach could well yield a courtroom-film corpus perfectly serviceable, from the critical perspective, as a genre. However, it would *not* yield a very good start-ing point for studying either the roots or the ramifications of automatic reflexivity. Nor—and here we pinpoint perhaps the most important result of the legal-genre experiment—does it yield an argument against doing so. By privileging genre, we do not account for or embrace auto-matic reflexivity, we leap-frog over it. An initial study of automatic reflexivity must not only look at a group of films and connect them to each other and to history but must historically position the unifying property itself.[16] While there is nothing "wrong" with studying the filmic courtroom (or any other law-in-film genre), studying such genres and studying *reflexivity* in films about law are two (or more) different things. There is a lot of overlap, of course, in the films one is likely to talk about. But whereas the courtroom genre is one of many genres and admits of a genre-theoretical approach based on approaches that also work with other genres, the automatic reflexivity of films about law is, I believe, sui generis, unique to the confluence of the legal and cin-ematic institutions from which it grows.

Instead of responding to the amorphous nature of the law-in-film corpus by redefining it until it lets us do genre criticism, let us follow the threads that resulted in the automatic reflexivity theory in the first place.[17] I propose that we can make theoretical sense of the properties of the law-in-film noncorpus even without our theory being one of genre; that what is involved shares some traits with the theoretical study of the underpinnings of genre; and that automatic reflexivity it-self resides among the underpinnings of the rigorous description of any possible *legal* film genres. Automatic reflexivity as a principle of theory is not like a genre but like *genre,* in the sense that it admits of—indeed, requires—a stepping back and opening up of the field of observation. In a sense, it functions as a parallel universe: just as Altman demonstrates that genre study requires its own critical equipment in matters such as history and textual analysis, so I would argue that automatic reflexivity requires its own built-in versions of these things.

Among the differences between genre study and a study of the auto-matic reflexivity of films about law is that the latter is probably not nearly as reusable as the former, simply because there are not very many cases of it.[18] On the other hand, as I hope to show here, the sweep of legal automatic reflexivity turns out to be considerable and to transect a number of different levels of theory, practice, history, and reception. This is not to say that Altman's approach results in a narrow field—far from it—but that the two enterprises discover depth along at least somewhat different axes.

Beyond the Syllogism: Elective Reflexivity

Films about law, I have suggested, are automatically reflexive; and, on this construction, they are *all* reflexive. As a category or framework for critical and historical inquiry, moreover, this reflexivity bears resemblances to, but differs from, the study of genre.

At the same time that we embrace the separation of genre from automatic reflexivity, we can also learn from genre study the lesson that there is a lot to say about these films and that it is important to move beyond the mere establishment of automatic reflexivity at the level of an on-off switch. Unless the entire matter of reflexivity in films about law goes beyond the automatic, it hardly qualifies as a tempting alternative critical framework to genre. According to the present argument, a film that includes a single shot of a policeman writing a parking ticket is reflexive, even if it contains no other references to legal process. In the absence of any mechanism for developing a more curious and elastic criticism, declaring such a film to be in the same company as *Day for Night* or *Veronika Voss* amounts to little more than a logic game.

In sum, the axiom of automatic reflexivity offers escape velocity from the notion of genre, but it also collapses or foreshortens a great deal of important variation among films that represent law. If all such films are reflexive in some inalienable sense, some of them nonetheless go a lot farther than others in cultivating and asserting their reflexivity—that is, in bringing to the surface the cluster of historical and narratological issues whose sharing by legal and filmic processes makes for automatic reflexivity in the first place. To predicate automatic reflexivity is to say little or nothing about films that dig their heels into plots about legal process, as opposed to those that sprint over it, and equally little about the changing historical currents that flow through and around films. I would continue to argue that even the most legally probing, thought-provoking film is reflexive, in the first instance, for precisely the same reason that the mythical film with one shot of a policeman is reflexive—namely, because it involves the representation of one narrative regime in the signifying terms of another. But the axiom of automatic reflexivity need not, and does not, hinder or take the place of a fuller critical reckoning with the more elaborate and sustained filmic treatments of law.

Here, as before, we may usefully turn to Altman's work on genre as a starting point. One of Altman's chief theoretical techniques is the exploration of the distinction between what he calls the *semantic* and the *syntactic* elements of a generic film. Broadly speaking, the semantic elements are the visible or audible tokens of a genre: cowboys in Westerns, singers in musicals, and so forth. Generic syntax has to do with how these tokens are combined and elaborated in ways that extend over time—both screen time (the narrative syntax of a given film as it relates to the use made of generic semantics) and film-historical time (changes in syntactic practices within a genre as that genre develops and responds to changing conditions in industry, social, and political history). The semantic/syntactic model of genre thus provides a way of looking at genre films along two perpendicular axes, as the static presence of tokens unfolds in their dynamic, "horizontal" use.

I would suggest that we can adapt the semantic/syntactic distinction for the particular type(s) of reflexivity we are talking about. In other words, automatic reflexivity might be called "semantic reflexivity"— a reflexivity brought about by the mere presence of certain tokens in the film (i.e., the tokens of legal process). Among other things, this terminology allows for an exploration of *syntactic* reflexivity; in other words, in addition to the static axiom that films about law are automatically or semantically reflexive, we carve out a space for observation and examination of the ways in which such films develop, beyond the level of axiom, a varied syntax of reflexive gestures.

While Altman's terms point us in the right direction, they are not a perfect fit for the particular case at hand. I will adhere to the term *automatic reflexivity* to refer to the static, universal reflexivity begotten by the presence of legal subject matter in films; and I will use the term *elective reflexivity* to refer to any filmic exploration of legal-narratological themes that goes beyond the automatic. Elective reflexivity is the reflexivity of films that dwell in the courtroom; whose plots actually hinge on legal issues; that put acts of legal storytelling at the center of dramatic crises; that engage the historical surrounds of their representations; and that bring to the surface the linkages and frictions among legal, cinematic, and representational problems attending the several institutions in question. To some extent, films of a high degree of elective reflexivity will correspond to those that might fit into the various law-film genres. But the correspondence is not complete. Given the reach of reflexivity as a critical instrument, it is possible to explore extrageneric films for their reflexive gestures: that is, relatively short courtroom scenes in films that do not belong to a courtroom genre may be of interest from the perspective of narrative theory and the relation between filmic and legal modes of representation.

Reflection and Refraction

The distinction between automatic and elective reflexivity provides a critical handle on the matter of how deeply or extensively a given film about law develops (or, in the critic's view, seems to develop) its reflexivity. This distinction alone would probably allow for at least a provisional taxonomy of films. However, it tells us relatively little about the *significance* of reflexivity in any particular case.

It has always been true that, far from being reflexive in an automatic or passive way, reflexive texts (at least important ones) are precisely those that most actively and obviously address the nature and conditions of their medium. Stam has occasion to address the point that reflexivity, even if driven by subject matter (or "automatic," in the present sense) in the first instance, may involve variation of degree. This point arises in his discussion of a particular type of reflexive film, namely, films about the making of films. Stam makes a case for a type of automatic reflexivity in the following terms: such films "necessarily entail a certain measure of reflexivity in that they foreground, in however indirect or idealized fashion, the institutional practices involved in their own production."[19] The very inclusion of a certain strain of subject matter constitutes, ipso facto, reflexivity.

In respect of method, this has resonances with the claim that the inclusion of legal subject matter in a film makes a film reflexive. Indeed, Stam is arguably on more instinctually solid ground than I am: positing an automatic or necessary reflexivity in the case of films-about-*film* has a more airtight quality than making the same claim for films-about-*law*. Yet, instructively, even in the context of the relatively robust films-about-film argument, Stam makes a point of avoiding a uniform or monolithic approach to the question of the significance of reflexivity. Films about the production of film "may treat this subject more or less critically, more or less reflexively, but they do have the virtue of reminding the reader or spectator that literary or filmic texts are products . . . mediated by complex commercial and cultural apparati."[20]

What Stam refers to as "more or less [critical], more or less [reflexive]" behavior on the part of texts corresponds fairly closely to what I have provisionally termed "syntactic reflexivity." The key point here is that taking the path of analyzing reflexivity, rather than genre, does not involve sacrificing a consideration of variability. Automatic reflexivity is a starting point, but there is more to it.[21]

Reflexivity in the arts, generally, implies a certain degree of dissent from traditional or mainstream modes and regimes of representation: that is, reflexive works turn their attention to aspects of their own life cycle (and to the life cycles of works in the same medium) that otherwise function discreetly in the service of illusionism. In cases where illusionism goes hand in hand with economic success, reflexive gestures often have the effect of suggesting or offering a critique, not only of the aesthetics involved, but of the economic and even political foundations on which those aesthetics rely and which, in turn, they reaffirm.

But if this is a typical pattern, it is not a necessary one. Reflexivity per se, however highly evolved, guarantees nothing in this regard. As Stam puts it:

> Texts may foreground the work of their signifiers or obscure it; the contrast cannot always be read as a political one. The reflexivity of *La Ronde* or *Singin' in the Rain* has little to do with leftist politics. . . . Or, to take an example from the realm of popular culture, commercial television is often reflexive and self-referential, yet that reflexivity is, to say the least, ambiguous. . . . The commercial interruptions that place programs on hold, for example, are not pauses for reflection but breaks for manipulation, intended not to make us think but to make us feel and buy. The self-referentiality of commercials that parody themselves or other commercials, similarly, are calculated to mystify rather than disenchant.[22]

In other words, even a film that goes in heavily for reflexivity can do so in a manner that is not particularly probing or critical. For instance, we may say that a courtroom scene that includes a film projector (such as the sequence in Fritz Lang's *Fury*) demonstrates a highly elective reflexivity: the apparatus appears literally. At the same time, such a scene need not rock the boat politically or ideologically; that is, even the literal presence *in* the fiction of the technology *behind* the fiction does not necessarily constitute an assault on the regime of representation at hand—or, in the case of law and film, either of the two regimes.

I will describe this as the distinction between *reflection* and *refraction*, where reflection means acquiescence in, or coming full circle to, the ideological status quo, and refraction means taking a position, or offering a point of view that involves some kind of real critique of, or dissent from, that ideology. The distinction between reflective and refractive texts does not coincide with the distinction between automatic and elective reflexivity. Rather, at least as a first approximation, we may say that a certain degree of elective reflexivity is a necessary but not sufficient condition of refraction—which is to say, first, that a film with a single shot of a traffic cop is unlikely to provide a significantly refractive view of the legal system; and, second, *even* a film that more elaborately draws out its reflexivity may nonetheless do no more than reflect that system's received values.

Thus we sketch out two continua: the automatic-elective and the reflective-refractive. It is important to bear in mind that, throughout the full ranges of both, we are in the realm of reflexivity, of which these pairs of terms describe different kinds and degrees; and that, in the case of any particular film, location along each of the continua may vary independently from placement along the other.

Courtroom Representation (Revisited) and the Typology of Reflexivity

All of the theoretical and historical points made up to this point—including the point about reflexivity—have to do with any legal process, including those of detection. At the same time, it seems to me that the courtroom has a privileged position in all of this. At the very least, it offers a rather massive sample pool, one that borders closely enough on a genre to keep things interesting while not quite falling into that category. The analogy between the rarified spaces of courtroom and cinema is very strong.

The courtroom scene makes perhaps the most compelling case for automatic reflexivity. While it may have seemed a stretch to claim reflexivity for the single shot of a traffic cop, it seems much more reasonable to argue that any scene in which the characters in a narrative film get together in one room to ask each other pointed questions about the story in progress is, whatever else it may be, reflexive. Courtroom scenes—without even trying—give center stage to the process of the construction of probabilistic narrative; they cannot abstain from referring, in some manner or at some level, to the underpinnings of both filmic and legal narrativity.

Wherever one draws the line between automatic and elective

reflexivities—never a clear line anyway—the courtroom film offers a range of both. Painting in very broad strokes, I submit that, overall, courtroom representation in film tends to demonstrate a high level of elective reflexivity or at least a strong pull in that direction. Elective reflexivity can take many forms in courtroom scenes, whether they are ideologically refractive or not. Film itself occasionally enters the courtroom, taking on the voice of a witness—as, for example, *Fury* or Stanley Kramer's *Judgment at Nuremberg.* The centrality of the verbal to courtroom procedure may be examined by cinematic means, which might involve counterverbal practices (up to and including silence) or, at the level of narrative construction, the implementation of flashback devices that result in oscillation between verbal and visual renderings of past events. A courtroom film can represent, and therefore examine, history—either specific historical events or historical conditions relevant to a particular time and place. And, in keeping with the global multiplicity of judicial practices and systems, a film may explore the relation between one such system and another—all superimposed on the representational system(s) of cinema.[23]

The filmic courtroom can host overt references to and embedded uses of filmic representation, as well as use what might be taken as disruptive and reflexive devices. But there is, once again, no necessary link between the implementation of such devices and any sense that the film is calling into question the underpinnings of either of the two narrative—or historical—institutions at whose confluence it stands. True of all filmic depictions of law, this is a key point in the case of the courtroom scene because its subject matter is irreducibly political.

The question of the political aspect of the reflexivity of the courtroom scene tends to merge with the more general question of the film's assumption of a critical stance toward the underlying processes of either or both of the two narrative institutions involved. There are, in other words, always political implications to its taking such a stance, and what concerns us here is the role of reflexivity in that process. Whatever boundaries we posit in these terms (and realizing that in most cases covered at this level of analysis we are not even on the margins of the issue of really overt or programmatic progressivism anyway), we can follow Stam's dismantling of the dichotomy by noting the important point that the mere presence of neither automatic nor elective reflexivity in the courtroom scene *necessarily* signals the operation of any kind of deeply probative critique of either the courtroom or the cinema. In other words, neither the flicking of the on-switch of auto-matic reflexivity nor the elaborations of elective reflexivity reliably betokens demystification—either of filmic illusionism or judicial veridicality. Thus the link is severed between reflexivity and the court-room scene's best and most native means of political expression: in the courtroom scene, narrative cannot avoid becoming concerned with narrative, but it need not do battle with the politics of narrativity.

Then again, it can. Courtroom representation provides tremendous opportunities for troubleshooting and critique of both legal and filmic narrativity and logomorphism, and many films cash in on the opportu-nity. Moreover, it is precisely in their treatments of logomorphism that ideologically reflective courtroom scenes tend to differ from refractive ones: when the refractive potential in a courtroom scene encounters an opposing pull, that pull comes consistently from the principle of ver-bal recountability. Courtroom scenes can absorb what might otherwise be an effective onslaught of reflexivity, specifically by turning the signifiers of disruption into grist for the verbal mill; or they can allow reflexivity full play.

The Pull of the Verbal   The courtroom is a hothouse of narrativity and a nonstop workshop in the craft of reconstituting antecedent truth through words. Therefore, the filmic courtroom is reflexive, and its very invocation—the very act of bringing these processes to the surface of a plot—constitutes a kind of rupture. To what extent this rupture matters evaluates to the question of its rededication to the principle of verbal recountability, the very principle that it has the potential to upend. Courtroom procedure in film, as elsewhere, operates in the thrall of the ultimate verbal distillate, the most implosive version—namely, the verdict. What does or does not happen on the way to the verdict can greatly vary.

Playfully reflexive filmic content is one thing; sustained critique of the logomorphic underpinnings of legal process is another; and the pres-ence of the former in a film does not invariably entail the presence of the latter. A courtroom scene may exhibit a significant degree of elec-tive reflexivity—formal devices that draw attention to the centrality of narrative, anti-illusionistic uses of, or even references to, filmic repre-sentation—while still not offering a refractive view of the regimes of narrative with which, in this manner, it plays. Analysis of such playful but nonradical scenes, moreover, generally reveals an overriding allegiance to the principle of logomorphism, a less than hasty, but nonetheless determined, journey toward the verdict.

An interesting example of formally reflexive behavior in the service of a rather nonrefractive goal is Herbert Wilcox's *Man Who Wouldn't Talk*, which concerns the murder trial of an (innocent) American government agent in England. At the beginning of the trial, the prosecutor addresses the jury, presenting the outline of the case against the defendant. Throughout the address he explains predictively what the jury will hear in the way of testimony from various witnesses. Each time he mentions a particular witness, however, that witness appears, shown in the witness box, superimposed in one corner of the screen next to the prosecutor's face; and with this "impossible" configuration on the screen, the prosecutor actually exchanges questions and answers with the witness.

This sequence utilizes filmic techniques that would normally be associated with dream representation or with a sustained, purposeful anti-illusionism: spatiotemporal integrity is smashed, a technical "trick" makes a mockery of the realist surface of the film, and so forth. In their context, however, the superimposed witnesses have no power as demystifiers but merely provide verbal discourse—testimony, proleptically obtained—which is fed into the forward-moving stream of the narrative under construction. The prosecutor is telling a story, as is the film. At this moment, the use of a disruptive visual device only contributes to the equilibrium and coherence of the emerging story, by verbal means; the formerly fanciful subserves the resolutely logomorphic. (It might be added that this film more broadly thematizes the generation of the coherent verbal narrative in that the protagonist pins his hopes on the English rule of law that a jury may stop a trial at any point where it feels it has enough evidence to reach a verdict—the suspense being generated in this case by the question of whether that point will be reached before the defendant is forced to reveal his spy-hood on the stand.)

Even when couched in electively reflexive visual language, then, law-in-film may in fact follow a logomorphic and veridical agenda. Another instance of this verbally compliant behavior of elective reflexivity in the filmic courtroom—a case in which the conquest of the anti-illusionistic gesture by the logomorphic takes more than one form—is provided by Lang's *Fury*. In establishing the physical presence of the defendants at the scene of the quasi-lynching of Joe, the prosecutor first coaxes perjurious alibis from various friends of the accused and then introduces filmic evidence that solidly refutes the witnesses' claims. This ploy is not only reflexive but science-fictional: a single newsreel camera produces an analytically edited compilation of evidence, complete with reverse-angle shots and continuity—visual, clear, and irrefutable.

At one level, the introduction of film into the courtroom of *Fury* would seem to suggest a rejection of the primacy of the principle of verbal recountability in the reconstitution of truth in favor of the "purely visual"; that is, it promises a refractive look at the matter of logomorphism in film and court by the conspicuously reflexive mechanism of film-in-court. Certainly the filmed sequences have no problem gainsaying the false witnesses, whom the prosecutor pointedly states will be charged with perjury. But the achievement of the newsreel nonetheless falls short of antiverbal triumph, in three respects.

First, the film is in a sense superfluous: it does not "know" anything that everyone else in the courtroom does not know. The only difference between it and the human witnesses is its readiness to be made to testify honestly. (In fact, a similar function is performed, in an abbreviated form, by the confession later in the trial of a conscience-stricken defendant.) It is not for the sake of troubleshooting the relationship between visuality and forensics that the film is enlisted as a witness but because it has a coercible voice.

Second, like many human witnesses in filmic and other courtrooms, the newsreel does not tell "the whole truth" in any of the imaginable conventional senses of that vacuous phrase. The prosecution uses the film to establish the whereabouts of the accused; later, when counsel for the defense finally gets around to mentioning that there is no evidence that a murder was committed, the film is mute. It can no more reveal the nonfruition of the lynching than can the human witnesses, all of whom think that Joe died during the assault on the jail. In spite of its different and practical qualities, the newsreel is by no means omniscient or transcendent in its vision.

Third, and most important, the use of the film-within-a-film in *Fury* does not constitute a disruptive moment in court because the trial still moves toward the verdict, the spoken word of truth, as its goal. The newsreel's visual testimony is thrown onto the same logomorph-destined conveyor belt as the verbal testimony of the flesh-and-blood witnesses. The prosecution's victory is not based on the ascendance of image over word but on the enlistment of *even* the image—and the fragmentary, inconclusive image, at that—to the ranks of collaborators in the distillation of the verdict.

In few arenas logically comparable to the filmic courtroom can so much reflexive play transmit so little critique, thanks to the effective granting in perpetuity of priority to the gravitational pull of the transcendental narrative referent and its chief material agent, the word. The courtroom film is always more film than courtroom; but when the story of the film and the story of the trial share a trajectory that favors a verbal basis, the reflexive moment finds itself disarmed and reappointed to a new and ideologically uncritical purpose. Not only may reflexivity be unconnected to institutional critique but, when such unconnectedness obtains in the case of the filmic courtroom, it is supplanted by a particularly ardent and telling adherence to the principle of verbal recountability, the lifeblood of both of the institutions brought together in the form.

Reflexivity in the Dock: The Courtroom of Comedy   One avenue of critical expression available to the filmmaker dabbling in courtroom representation is comedy. Moreover, comedy often presents something of a shortcut to reflexivity; here, it will serve us in that capacity, allowing for a relatively expeditious look at a few further aspects of the reflexive courtroom.

Self-evidently, directorial recourse to the comic courtroom does not in and of itself signal a counterideological stance or a subversive text. In this respect, comedy follows—and is often subsumed by—the general patterns of reflexivity in courtroom scenes. The crisis presented in *Miracle on 34th Street*, for example, is resolved as the "brilliant lawyer" figure points out in court that the United States Post Office has forwarded Santa Claus's mail to his client; therefore, the government has officially recognized his client as Santa Claus. However witty this fantastic maneuver is (and opinion on this point may well vary), it is ultimately affirmative of, rather than dissident from, the ideological basis of justice in the textual properties of the convincing and structurally perfect narrative.

We move into considerably more ambivalent territory with *Gentlemen Prefer Blondes*. At the very least, Dorothy (Jane Russell) commits perjury rather grandly and gets away with it, actually impersonating Lorelei Lee (Marilyn Monroe) on the witness stand. (From the perspective of genre study, it is noteworthy that although this is a musical, and therefore a fictional milieu in which spontaneous song is the norm, Dorothy's breaking into song *in the courtroom* takes people by surprise and is interpreted as disruptive and out of place.) Courtroom ceremony and law are swept aside in the interest of Dorothy's plans. The catch, if it may be called that, is of course that the overriding purpose to which judicial decorum finds itself sacrificed and narrative teleology lampooned is the very unrefractive one of the establishment of happy and stable married couples.

For a considerably more involved example of the critical potential of the comic courtroom, let us turn to a third example, namely, Woody Allen's *Bananas*. The courtroom sequence in *Bananas* lends itself to a double traversal by a theory of reflexivity. The first of the scene's two reflexive threads, or modes of reflexivity elaborated in it, involves the judicial process of the construction of a coherent and adequate narrative, the teleology of whose narration mandates a narrow and "relevant" path through an infinite field of available or potential utterances. The courtroom of *Bananas* is a synoptic rubbish heap, both a collection of fragments from judicial narratives and a minitaxonomy of fragmentable narrative types. Throughout, any sign or possibility of the easy or predictable crystallization of narrative terms about a stable and integral referent is repelled. Logomorphism does not have an easy time of it.

Many mundane elements of courtroom procedure appear in the scene—enough to account for a fairly ample and well-stocked filmic trial—but in a disconnected way, without the classical consistencies among narratives and versions. Over and over, the acts of courtroom drama are performed, but the acts themselves are randomized and scattered, as if pulled together from many trials (or even from many parodic trial scenes). A man bursts into the courtroom and, facing the judge from the gallery, emotionally confesses; it turns out that he has burst into the wrong room. Fielding Mellish (Allen) cross-examines a police officer who has testified against him—in accordance with procedure, but with a somewhat irrelevant question (to wit: "Officer Dowd, have you ever had sexual relations with a girl with really big breasts?").[24] Bound and gagged, Mellish cross-examines another witness and, his words unintelligible but his manner that of the hostile attorney out for blood, reduces her to confession and tears.

In each of these instances, the forward motion of the trial scene escapes the constraints of logomorphism—whether by the mechanism of coherent but utterly irrelevant narrative or that of incoherent noises functioning unchallenged in the place of articulate sounds. A final example from the scene is perhaps the most strikingly critical of the logomorphic tendency in the construction of an inferred truth in court. A character witness for Mellish says, "I'm sorry to disappoint you, but I've known Fielding Mellish for years and he's a warm, wonderful human being." "Would the clerk read that statement back, please?" requests Mellish. "I've known Fielding Mellish for years," the clerk reads, "and he is a rotten, conniving, dishonest little rat." "O.K.," says Mellish; "I just wanted to make sure you were getting it." So much, we might surmise, for the pull of the word, metaphysical connectedness among multiple versions, and the ostensible subjugation of representation to its essential source.

The courtroom sequence of *Bananas* throws a challenge to the mighty force of the narrative referent at the level of its representation in sanctified and dignified verbal activity. As I stated earlier, I take this as the first of two threads of refractive reflexivity running through the scene. The second has a different relation to narrative theory. In fact, it opens out onto a new facet of narrative: the narrativity of the body.

This is the theme—at play throughout the film, and quite concentrated and distilled in the courtroom—of multiple identity, disguise, and impersonation. Allen, of course, went on to explore this theme far more richly in *Zelig*; but it is nonetheless one of the central motifs of *Bananas*. Investigating the intertextuality and reflexivity of *Zelig*, Robert Stam and Ella Shohat have dubbed that film a "chameleon text,"[25] and perhaps (if the expression is not too biologically literal) the instability of identity in *Bananas* affords a glimpse at the chameleon in embryo.

What is involved here is a shift in the registers of stability and change. Courtroom procedure, like film, involves role playing: judge, defendant, witness, and so forth, are templates or placeholders into which specific identities are plugged. In *Bananas*, this is taken to a further, and refractive, level: not only officially sanctioned roles but entire identities are passed, like masks, from face to face. Identity, name, and position float freely from the body in a new and unstable play of legal theater.

With the hindsight of the Zelig character, Mellish can be looked at—in theoretical raking light, so to speak—as something of a trial run for the later, more mature chameleon. To begin with, the plot of *Bananas* involves rather centrally Mellish's return, incognito, from San Marcos to the United States. There are other signs as well of the instability of his identity, manifested both in an undirected, general sense of misfit-tedness (in his job and his social life) and in a few incidents of quasi-Zeligian adaptation—particularly his being pushed into the role of sur-geon by his father, as well as his tendency to court Nancy by trying to discuss things that interest her, adopting her political causes, and en-gaging in her activities. In his own way, Mellish can slip in and out of character(s), and in and out of the periphery of his own world, with the best of them.

Instability of identity thwarts the ideology of conformity, and the courtroom sequence of *Bananas* mocks that ideology—conformity of vision, opinion, speech, body. Miss America condemns Mellish because his views differ from those of the president and others of his kind; that is, Mellish fails to see with the eyes of the presidential mask. J. Edgar Hoover appears in the guise of a black woman ("I have many enemies"); and Mellish examines himself on the witness stand, filling the roles of witness and attorney at the same time. Identity slips, masks are passed around; the players of roles are themselves taken up bodily into the game of story and narrativity, not now as devices of event replication, but as playing pieces, as in a game of human chess not quite under the players' control.

"Machines hate me," laments Mellish near the beginning of the film (in an utterance that stands as motto for the film's entire *Modern Times* agenda), and none more than the machine of judicial narrative. The film's layered comedy consistently takes the form of referentially im-possible or ironic pairings: the testimony changed as it is repeated ver-batim, the right climax to the wrong narrative, the body pressed into double service, the right-wing luminary behind the eyes of the minor-ity member. It is more than a wrench in the machine (cf. *Gentlemen Prefer Blondes*); rather, it is a vision of a new machine, built on the same blueprint as the old but in the absence of an acquiescent and logomorphic vision, like the mixed-up rifle Mellish misconstructs—blindfolded, no less—during his training in the rebel camp.

Afterthoughts on Textual Determinism

The sequence of films considered above—*The Man Who Wouldn't Talk/Fury/Bananas*—illustrates a range of possible relations among some of the major building blocks of law-in-film: on-screen duration, logomorphism, elective reflexivity, and reflection versus refraction of the underlying institutional ideology. In particular, it illustrates the fact that these elements vary independently: long screen time in court does not equate to a refractive take on law; the presence of cameras in the court does not equate to a sustained unmasking of traditional illusionistic film techniques; and so forth. We have moved beyond the realm of axiom, in other words—beyond the stipulation that films representing law are automatically reflexive—and started to consider how, and to what effect, one film's reflexivity may differ from another's.

In crossing that line from axiom to critique, we encounter the question of textual versus authorial versus critical determination—that is, the question of exactly who or what (creator? "the film"? viewer?) is electing all this more evolved reflexivity. In general, reflexivity has the quality of being driven or, arguably, created in the act of viewing or reading. In other words, it can be in the eye of the beholder; in fact, it must at least be that. As with all matters of textual determinism, there is a range of possibilities: everything from a reflexivity that the author planned but the reader did not see, to one that the reader, but not the author, understood. There is no rigid way to determine how much reflexivity is intentional and how much projected by the viewer—that is, no criteria equivalent to the grammatical rules governing reflexive verbs. For instance, my own interpretation of the 1985 made-for-television movie *Stone Pillow*, which stars Lucille Ball, is that it is a reflexive look at Ball's earlier career. The movie features Ball as a homeless woman mourning her previous life and the husband and son who were part of it—a reference, at least in my mind, to *I Love Lucy* and its status as the high point of Ball's television career. Further research might or might not reveal this reflexive gesture to have been creatively planned; but it strongly influenced my understanding of the movie and thus, as a matter of critical response, was "there."

Different respondents to a film will see different things; one may see nothing, while another sees a profound critique of justice. Indeed, this relativity of filmic meaning to the instance of viewing goes well beyond the matter of law in film. Meaning is, at most, only partially textually determined. There is always a fault line running through textual criticism and analysis, and such criticism is always, in some degree, confessional. At the same time, there is such a thing as getting too precious about this, or too absorbed in it, at the expense of forward motion in the act of critical writing itself. An awareness of the contingency of meaning need not evaluate to the nonperformance of criticism. If—to reason from analogy—we go to the concert hall and hear a violinist, we may completely understand that his performance represents a very personal interpretation. We may even believe that the music he is playing gains its profundity only relative to a certain culture or a certain historical tradition, outside of which the experience of hearing it would be trivial. But we do not expect the violinist, for all that, to stop playing and lecture the audience on the cultural contingency of music.

Similarly, an awareness of the relativity of criticism to the traditions that host it should not lead us to reject it. The trap for textual critics (as opposed to violinists) is the continuity of form: we are writing, whether about the topic at hand or about the fact that our position on that topic is relative and critic-determined. The fact that both of these types of discourse involve writing makes the transition from one to the other too easy and obscures the fact that it is possible to be extremely relativistic and, nonetheless, to participate in a rhetorical practice whose significance we understand to be relative.

Accordingly, I choose not to deny the presence of this fault line but rather to redistribute the stress and get on with the enterprise. On offer here, in other words, is a critical framework, a filter through which the representation of legal processes in film may be viewed.

Notes

1. Robert Stam, *Reflexivity in Film and Literature from Don Quixote to Jean-Luc Godard* (Ann Arbor: University of Michigan Press, 1985).

2. Ibid., 32.

3. Ibid.

4. Ibid., 43.

5. Ibid.

6. One way to clarify the notion of automatic reflexivity is to look for it in other bodies or types of films. An interesting pair of examples is the Western and the musical. No doubt there is such a thing as a reflexive Western; in fact, a fair amount of Western-related scholarship and analysis has to do with various strains of self-awareness and deliberate genre revisionism in the form. Such gestures are reflexive. However, the vast majority of this reflexivity consists of the Western genre feeding on itself, on the history of its own *films*, rather than on external, third-party themes or devices.

Musicals, by way of contrast, arguably exhibit something very close to automatic reflexivity. Very broadly, the musical numbers in a musical are either accounted for by the plot—that is, part of a plotted performance, such as a musical-within-the-musical or quasi-public performance, as in *The Sound of*

Music—or not. In the former case, the presence of performance within the plot of the film constitutes at least a type of reflexivity, given that the film itself is performative. In the latter case—when musical numbers erupt into the text without justification in the plot—a case might be made, too, for reflexivity, since the actors' bursting into song outside the logic of the plot is anti-illusionistic and strange. (Except, of course, that it isn't "strange" if you're used to it. I am thus indulging in some fairly oversimplified reception theory, as well as genre theory, for the sake of mapping out the contours of my more detailed arguments.)

7. Paul Bergman and Michael Asimow, *Reel Justice: The Courtroom Goes to the Movies* (Kansas City, Mo.: Andrews and McMeel, 1996).

8. Alex Kozinski, "Foreword," in ibid., xi.

9. Bergman and Asimow, 100.

10. Rick Altman, *The American Film Musical* (Bloomington: Indiana University Press, 1987).

11. Ibid., 1.

12. In general, I have a distaste for "applying" an author's theories to a new text or body of texts. The very idea makes less sense than its popularity would suggest; the results, more often than not, are as predictable and unchallenging as the approach is formulaic. Furthermore, the theory-application algorithm has contributed to the unfortunate establishment of a small and overworked pantheon of writers (Foucault, Barthes, Lacan, and so forth) and has placed obstacles in the path of theory itself. Contemporary scholarship in the humanities has the ring of a convention of ventriloquists, each propping up the inanimate form of a theorist and attempting to speak through it.

I hope that my recourse to Altman's work does not fall into this category. For one thing, Altman explicitly includes intellectual reuse and sharing among his purposes in *The American Film Musical*; he writes of "enfranchising" other and future scholars of genre. This is really the thrust of the whole genre-theory agenda of the book, and—not unimportantly—he does it well. Furthermore, I intend to keep my encounter with Altman quite cannibalistic. My purpose here is to explore the implications of a theory of automatic reflexivity for the study of the cultural and scholarly convergences between law and film. The entire project of borrowing a perspective and a methodology from Altman serves that purpose and will only be sustained to the extent that it does so.

13. Ibid., 12–13.

14. Ibid., 13.

15. In exploring the process Altman outlines, I am begging the question of Hollywood versus non-Hollywood films—a question that would have to play a much more central role in a really thorough treatment of courtroom films *as a genre.*

16. This might seem to suggest, since it is in the context of looking at Altman's work, that there is some level of historical contextualizing that Altman does not aim for or achieve—which is not true. Altman peels back every imaginable layer of preconception and historical contingency, but his work (at least this particular book) is explicitly metacritical. My point is that we could follow his lead and come up with extremely robust genre analyses and genre-historical discussions that nonetheless, in the case of films about law, would not stand in the same relation to the fact of genre as this work stands in relation to the fact of automatic reflexivity.

17. These spatial metaphors—following, going backward—emphasize the fact that the work underway here does not stand in an adversarial position with respect to genre criticism but swerves in and out of contact with it. Indeed, I imagine that someday someone will write an excellent study of the various law-in-film genres. I hope that person finds some useful theoretical and historical arguments here.

18. Films about film might lend themselves to a study of this kind, involving aspects of the relationship between theory and practice.

19. Stam, 71.

20. Ibid.

21. Stam's work includes some interesting further crossing of paths between the notions of reflexivity and genre—in particular, the third chapter of *Reflexivity in Film and Literature*, which is entitled "The Genre of Self-Consciousness." That chapter is concerned primarily with spelling out many of the techniques of production, narrative organization, and anti-illusionism deployed by reflexive writers and filmmakers. The genre treated by the chapter is thus defined not by content or subject matter but by authorial strategy and its positioning in the history of narrative. Interestingly, Stam puts the very term "genre" on the other side of the fence before redeeming it for reflexivity: "In their freedom and creativity, anti-illusionistic artists imitate the freedom and creativity of the gods. Like gods at play, reflexive artists see themselves as unbound by life as it is perceived (Reality), by stories as they have been told (Genre), or by a nebulous probability (Verisimilitude)" (129).

Stam's notion of genre straddles neighboring levels of abstraction: it can be a function of narrative tradition, repetition, and constraint (e.g., the thematic elements of a Western); or it can be the aggregation over time, and between art forms, of refusals of such constraints and dismemberings of such traditions. While there is probably a diminishing return on minutely reconciling Stam's usage and mine, one way to describe the way I am using reflexivity is that it corresponds more closely to what Stam calls "genre" than to what he calls "Genre."

22. Ibid., 16.

23. I will take up this thread—the matter of one entire system of law brought into conflict with another, in filmic representation—in chapter 8.

24. Throughout this book, all direct quotations from films and television programs were transcribed by the author during viewings.

25. See Robert Stam and Ella Shohat, "*Zelig* and Contemporary Theory: Meditation on the Chameleon Text," *Enclitic* 9.1–2 (1987): 176–93.

4

History, Genre, and Reflexivity

Rick Altman's theoretical approach to genre goes somewhere; specifically, it goes to the matter of genre history. From the start—that is, from the point of outlining the phases of genre study prior to carrying out his detailed study of the musical—Altman positions genre-historical analysis as a late phase of the process and a culminative one at that: "Once a final corpus has been established, the question of genre history can no longer be avoided."[1]

History plays a role, too, in the process of examining the relationships between law and film in the framework I am developing here. Its role is not the same as the role Altman assigns to it in the area of genre study, but in this matter, as elsewhere, Altman's treatment of genre can serve as a productive and challenging point of reference and departure. In fact, we have already seen an important example—or perhaps "stratum" would be a better word—of historical context for the entire phenomenon of automatic reflexivity in films about law: namely, the status of narrative as historically documentable choice for the role of central organizing principle. Automatic reflexivity itself is an effect of this choice, a theoretical peg on which to hang the product of two historically contingent factors.

Here already there is a parallel with the notion of genre history in the widest sense. Genre itself has a history and a historically contingent development as an organizing principle of the production, consumption, and study of clusters of texts. However, the process of refining the field of study, from this broadest level to the next, differs as between genre and automatic reflexivity. One can say: genre is historically contingent, and so is the musical. However, there is no exactly equivalent pair of statements for films-about-law as understood here. (The sustained example of the provisional courtroom genre was useful for certain analytical purposes, but at the same time it was an analysis of elective rather than automatic reflexivity.) There is no exact equivalent to the "genre/*a* genre" relationship when the first term in the pair is "the automatic reflexivity of films about law."

If this transition is missing, then all the more difficult to specify is the next: "a genre/a film." This means that the analysis of any particular film-about-law, *as an automatically reflexive film*, stands in a different relation to its most broadly defined theoretical environment than does any given genre film. Films-about-law cluster together and stand as a theoretical entirety under the rubric of automatic reflexivity. But at any subsequent order of magnification, they cluster very loosely, if at all.

The risk in developing the theoretical model through various stages is the risk of excessive formalism and inadequate historicization.[2] The "floating" of films within a vast space, whose only delimiter is a rather grand theoretical axiom, can lead to a floating style of historical positioning. I would like to explore ways of avoiding this ahistoricalism, while not losing sight of the historical contingency of the whole thing. On the one hand, given that the grouping of films on the macrocriterion of automatic reflexivity *already* positions them historically, any subsequent analysis that develops in line with it, even if formalist in style, already has a historical component. To that extent, the whole notion of automatic reflexivity, itself historical, boosts us over the hurdle of historicality. On the other hand, whether in the analysis of one film or a provisional coupling or clustering of films, automatic reflexivity is unlikely to be the *entire* answer to the question of historical resonance and place.

A Case Study: *In a Lonely Place*

A First Traversal   As a case study in these issues of inclusiveness, singularity, and history, I will turn in some detail to Nicholas Ray's 1950 film *In a Lonely Place*, which deals quite directly with the perplexities of storytelling and legal process and, I will argue, somewhat indirectly but no less centrally with very specific matters of history.[3]

In a recent monograph on the film, Dana Polan has made an interesting case for understanding *In a Lonely Place* as standing at the confluence of several distinct film genres. Its status as film noir never in doubt, Polan argues, the film also exhibits nontrivial characteristics of the screwball comedy and the woman's Gothic film:

> Most immediately, *In a Lonely Place* has much of the wisecracking approach to love that we find in the screwballs (for instance, when Dix tells Laurel they'll have dinner together, she replies that certainly they'll both have dinner, but not together). . . . *In a Lonely Place* also echoes the screwball film's feeling that resorting to tricks and strategies in matters of love is justified if they bring the loved one out of a limited way of life. . . .
>
> . . . [T]he dangers for Dix are much less significant than those confronted by Laurel, who has to wonder directly if the man in her life is a murderer. In this respect . . . it might also be productive to treat the film as a late example of another 40s genre, important for its thoughts on love and suspicion in the amorous couple: the female Gothic film, in which a woman wonders about the designs upon her of the man in her life—does he love her, does he hate her, does he wish to do her harm?[4]

Somewhat in the spirit of Polan's multigenre take on the film, I would suggest that *In a Lonely Place* also exhibits a number of different and identifiable (if not entirely separable) strains of reflexivity. To begin with, the film is set in Hollywood and fully cashes in on this self-referential premise. *Noir* (i.e., ambivalent) protagonist Dixon Steele (Humphrey Bogart) is a screenwriter; lover Laurel Gray (Gloria Grahame) is an aspiring actress; and the plot revolves largely around the professional milieu of film production. This intimacy between text and production process reaches even higher levels (or perhaps lower, depending on how one calibrates it): famously, Nicholas Ray and Gloria Grahame were married but had separated by the time of the production of *In a Lonely Place*.[5]

Even these examples of Hollywood reflexivity might admit of further subdivision (personal, professional, promotional), but by leaving them aggregated under the Hollywood label, we may distinguish another area of reflexivity—namely, reflexivity pertaining to acts of storytelling and narration. As Polan points out, the film is replete with acts of storytelling and even references to such acts: Mildred Atkinson telling the story of *Althea Bruce* to Dix; Dix telling Brub and Sylvia his version of the murder narrative (about which I will say more presently); Dix's professional activity in general and several pointedly story-connected lines in particular ("It was his story against mine. Of course, I told my story better"; the association of storytelling with sexuality in the wisecrack of Fran, Dix's former lover: "Remember when you used to tell me stories?"). Stories are told, and some of those stories are stories about the tellings of stories. Furthermore, many of the more pivotal acts of narrating in the film involve, specifically, slippage and comparison among different versions and registers of expression: book and screenplay, legal and imaginative narrative. The result is a plurality of parallel and at times overlapping narrative teleologies: finishing the screenplay, finishing the legal investigation, finishing the film.

Storytelling is also associated with authorial power in *In a Lonely Place*, understood in this connection as a sibling, or arguably an ancestor, of legal power. Battles of several kinds are waged on the field of narrative—not the least of these being Lockner's investigation of the murder of Mildred Atkinson, an investigation whose prejudicial view of Dix drives the whole film but which nonetheless consists of putting together a legally admissible story. In his capacity as screenwriter—literal, professional author—Dix despises the novel *Althea Bruce* and makes significant changes to the story in adapting it for the screen. (There is an interesting reflexivity even about this gesture of artistic authority: the film *In a Lonely Place* itself departs in several substantive ways from the original novel by Dorothy B. Hughes, most notably in the fact that the Dixon Steele of the novel is guilty of murder, while the film's Dixon is not.)[6] These changes to *Althea Bruce* become the focal point of the issues of the screenplay's acceptance by Brodie, the producer—authority figure—and thus bear directly on Dix's chances for economic stability. Literal authorship, authorial voice, and authority converge everywhere.

Storytelling joins up with what can best be described as military power in a scene frequently alluded to for the extremity of its lighting but important for extremity of several kinds: namely, the scene in which Dix, a dinner guest at the home of Brub and Sylvia Nicolai, dramatizes his theory about the murder of Mildred by staging a reenactment of it, with Brub and Sylvia, sitting side by side as Mildred and the murderer would have been in the car, in the leading roles. Dix sits opposite the couple (bathed in the famous extreme light) and coaches—*directs*—the action. As Dix describes his vision of the murder, partly as present-tense narrative and partly as instructions to the couple, Brub follows his orders and comes uncomfortably close to choking Sylvia. In part, Dix's authorial power here—that is, the power to coerce the material world around him through the instrument of narrative—serves to point up Brub's perennial and unquestioning willingness to

take orders; as a function of the portrayal of Brub's character throughout the film, this is the same tendency that leads him to betray his
friendship with Dix at the instigation of his boss, Captain Lockner.

At the same time, Dix's authorial/narratorial control of Brub echoes
the wartime relationship between the two men: Dix was Brub's commanding officer. This disturbing example of the survival of a military
mentality (and relationship) into civilian life, in turn, joins up with a
number of other uneasy references to the war and its legacy. Dix has
not had a hit (in the cinematic sense) since before the war, and his rap
sheet, as recited by Lockner, begins in 1946. Robert Sklar suggests that
In a Lonely Place "refuses to credit professional failure, a veteran's maladjustment, or Hollywood as specific causes of [Dix's] anger and violence."[7] But a pattern does emerge with respect to the war—perhaps not
exactly a causal relationship, but at least a relationship of favorable
conditions (maladjustment in general, the lingering authority over Brub
in particular) and tangible consequences. There is no extrapolating a
fully developed position on the politics of World War II from the film;
but there does seem to be a fairly direct line drawn between the phenomenon of wartime authority and the destructive power of that authority—out of its element, wayward—in civilian life.

Connected as it may be with matters of authorial and even directorial power, the film's sustained indictment of these war-derived effects
also constitutes an aspect of its *historical* reflexivity. Indeed, there is
even more overlap and concatenation than this among the ostensible
categories of reflexivity I am mapping out here ("Hollywood" is "historical" too). But, beyond the war theme, there is one historical point
of reference in particular at work in the film, a reference important
enough to merit its own category: namely, the unspoken but deeply
determining theme of cold war domestic politics and the entire matter
of the House Un-American Activities Committee (HUAC). Putting it
somewhat abstractly, *In a Lonely Place* is a film written and produced
in 1949 whose story revolves around the unjust persecution of a Hollywood screenwriter. The screenwriter's best friend doubles as informant;
and his career in Hollywood is in the balance. His lover does what she
can to stonewall the authorities.[8]

The fit between the film's disposition of legal investigation and the
history of HUAC in Hollywood might be called allegory—and an allegorical interpretation might stretch it even farther than I have here.[9]
But at key points of contact, the fit between the film and history is too

exact to be taken comfortably as allegory. A story about a Hollywood screenwriter unjustly accused of murder hardly qualifies as an allegory of HUAC persecution of Hollywood personnel. The matter has been taken a step beyond allegory, analogy, or parable.

The historical interest of *In a Lonely Place* meets up with the narratological interest and the matter of the representation of law—that representation, on the construction presented here, spanning the manifest plot and the legal host environment of the film's time (the presence of HUAC in Hollywood). History in relation to reflexivity differs from genre history, not because the latter can have nothing to say about such relationships, but because the former does not necessarily add up to the history of anything. It need not lack precision or depth, but it has (at least sometimes) an atomic quality to it. For example, this analysis of *In a Lonely Place* might or might not have a bearing on other films noir. It might have more to do with science fiction or alien-invasion movies, which (in their own way) also treat the matter of communist infiltration in more or less allegorical, more or less transfigured terms. *In a Lonely Place* might also be understood as an important antecedent of all subsequent films *explicitly* about HUAC in Hollywood. The point is that however we concatenate the film historically in relation to other films, the idea of looking at it as a film about legal process (investigation, interrogation, determination of innocence) invites us to look at it historically, in several senses, even if we thereby cut it adrift from one or more of its genres.

A Second Traversal   The reflexive gestures of *In a Lonely Place* may also be characterized according to the critical framework already at hand—that is, the identification of automatic and elective reflexivities in films about law and the distinction between the refractive and the reflective use of those reflexivities. To begin with, of course, the film includes characters who are legal investigators, and its plot revolves around legal investigation; it thus exhibits the automatic reflexivity of the film about law. *In a Lonely Place* exhibits, too, the extended and visible treatment of reflexive elements characteristic of elective reflexivity. The whole matter of Dixon's involvement with storytelling, professional and otherwise, amounts to an elective elaboration of the underlying, axiomatic reflexivity connected more simply with there being a legal "story" in the first place. In other words, the film does not leave matters of narrative and narrativity aside, nor are they subsumed in a perfunctory inclusion of legal plot material; rather, it explores them in a sustained and complex manner.

In a Lonely Place is a refractive film. That is, to the extent that *In a Lonely Place* displays an elective reflexivity (an inclusion of and visible reckoning with the underpinnings of legal, verbal, and even filmic representation), it does so in the service of a critical and nonacquiescent take on the processes it represents. If Dixon's being a screenwriter is an example of elective reflexivity, his being a screenwriter persecuted for a crime he did not commit—understood in the context of HUAC—is an example of refraction: the *use* of elective reflexivity in the area of the representation of legal processes to say something about, in this case, history and the problematic sides of the law.

If refraction, as I have outlined it, has something to do with a film's refusal to be politically inert, and if what we are looking at (or for) is specifically a nonreflective, nonacquiescent view of the unjust persecution that was visited on Hollywood around the time of the making of the film, then the key figure in *In a Lonely Place* is Captain Lockner. Wrongly convinced of the guilt of Dix, Lockner has stepped into Dix's shoes in that he is Brub's postwar "commanding officer." The film plays up the question of Brub's divided loyalties but with a rather clear orientation toward friendship and away from unthinking obedience to menacing authority figures. Lockner's suspicion of Dix, which he succeeds in passing on to Laurel, rests largely on Dix's manifest social differentness and the improbably mordant cadence of his speech: in short, Dix is strange and rude. But where Lockner's suspicion finds no nourishment in Dix's strangeness, it switches gears and looks instead to the normality of others: Lockner shows Laurel a number of mug shots of killers and, challenging her to notice that they all look like normal people, reasons that even disagreement as to Dix's strangeness cannot exonerate Dix. Once again, we seem to be in textbook witch-hunt territory.

The film's celebrated lack of closure with respect to culpability, in a sense that goes beyond the killing of Mildred (or has nothing to do with it in the first place), is another example of its refractive treatment of history. The scene in question is the last one in the film. Violently jealous, Dix attacks Laurel, who has grown fearful of him (based not only on the Mildred enigma but also on reports of his past violence and her own witnessing of it) and whom Dix has discovered to be planning to leave him.[10] What I have called "unjust persecution" is not the persecution of the entirely blameless; nor are we presented with a "means justifying the end" conundrum, as in the case of Orson Welles's *Touch of Evil*, which depicts the illegal framing for murder of a man who turns out to be guilty. *In a Lonely Place* has much to do with the separation between public and private life and the dangers specific to the failure of that separation—even when the private life in question is not a particularly innocent one.

This double traversal of the film on criteria of reflexivity suggests several things. First, it is perfectly possible to analyze a film like *In a Lonely Place* as a reflexive film using ad hoc categories of reflexivity such as "Hollywood" and "narratological." Second, the use of the more abstract categories under development here—automatic, elective, reflective, refractive—can still give us something to say and can provide points of contact with other films whose reflexivity may not take the same thematic forms but may admit of comparison at the functional level represented by these categories. Third, the approach based around the levels of reflexivity of films about law may involve a fairly high degree of abstraction, but it is not, in and of itself, ahistorical; nor does it close the door on any historical observation, in the case of this or that particular film. What it does is to straddle a number of important topics and themes, of which history is one, and provide criteria on which, specifically, films about law may be examined and compared.

I have been at pains to examine the relationship between my approach and both genre and reflexivity in general, in part because what I am doing here has much in common with past theoretical work in those areas and in part to suggest what might be different, and significant, about a study grounded in automatic reflexivity and the behaviors that either do or do not grow out of it. If reflexivity in films about law is indeed automatic or axiomatic, then films about law that do not cash in on their reflexivity—that do not elaborate on or through it— become visible for not doing so. Elective reflexivity may be understood as an opportunity of which advantage either is or is not taken; and if this is a formalistic way of looking at the matter, the matter being so looked at is nonetheless deeply historical and historically connected.

Notes

1. Rick Altman, *The American Film Musical* (Bloomington: Indiana University Press, 1987), 14.

2. I say "excessive formalism" rather than "formalism" because I do not believe that all formalism is bad, nor even that all formalism is ahistorical or antihistorical.

3. The briefest of plot summaries follows; readers are encouraged to view the film itself, a masterpiece only recently beginning to receive the kind of attention it deserves from critics and historians. Screenwriter Dixon Steele (Humphrey Bogart), without a hit since before World War II, invites hatcheck girl Mildred Atkinson to his house so that she can recount to him the plot of the potboiler *Althea Bruce*, which he may be adapting for the screen (specifically, for a never-seen producer named Brodie). Mildred is murdered on her way home. Dixon meets Laurel Gray, an aspiring actress who lives across the courtyard; they fall in love, meeting formally for the first time at police headquarters, where Laurel serves as Dix's alibi, having spotted him across the way at the very time when Mildred was being murdered. Sergeant Lockner is not convinced and pursues the case against Dix—with the help of Detective Brub Nicolai, a friend and former military underling of Dix. Ultimately, Dix is cleared, but not before irreparable damage has been done to his relationship with Laurel.

4. Dana Polan, *In a Lonely Place* (London: British Film Institute, 1993), 17, 20–21. The dinner line ("We'll have dinner tonight, but not together"), which Polan connects with the film's screwball-ish side, also weighs in on the noir side of things. The film is full of dialogue suggesting dislocation, nonmeeting of minds, and a kind of "off-by-one" cognitive relationship between speakers. (Dix, to former girlfriend Fran: "I was pretty nice to you." Fran: "No, not *to* me. But you were pretty nice.")

5. Ibid., 19–20.

6. See Polan (esp. pp. 26–30) for an extended treatment of the relationship between the novel and the film.

7. Robert Sklar, *City Boys: Cagney, Bogart, Garfield* (Princeton, N.J.: Princeton University Press, 1992), 235.

8. Interestingly, Sklar makes much the same point about Santana Productions' next film, *Sirocco*, but not about *In a Lonely Place*. Of *Sirocco*, Sklar writes: "Among the political issues raised in the film is the question of informing: it is difficult to believe this is merely a coincidence in a film made in late 1950 with additional scenes shot in March 1951, at the time of the renewed HUAC hearings" (ibid., 237).

9. Laurel as allegory of the Committee for the First Amendment, perhaps . . . As I say, a stretch.

10. At one point, the screenplay had Dix murdering Laurel at the end. Polan suggests that there is even reason to believe that this alternate ending was filmed.

Part 3

Regimes of Writing

5

Metaphorical Bridges

Plenty of writings about law and film present themselves quite candidly and without the need for a lot of subtle or subterranean searching. But subtle and subterranean searching produces an interesting yield, too. In fact, two of the three chapters comprising this part will reflect such searching—namely, this chapter and chapter 7.

Here, the focus is on ways in which writings about film and law have established and explored connections between the two areas of a metaphorical and/or analogical kind. A small number of such connections figure in more or less common parlance: the camera as witness, the critic as judge. A little bit of lexical fancy can go a long way toward adding to the list: viewer as judge; film as defendant; spectator as spectator; critic as jury; jury as viewer; bailiff as usher; gavel as clapboard; and so on. Choosing a middle ground between rehashing the clichés and straining the fancy, I will concentrate here on particular aspects of two figures, the witness and the detective, around whom some intriguing metaphorical criticism has developed. Much of what has emerged so far from our consideration of film and law as parallel regimes is an ambivalence about narrative and language, and the key analogical and metaphorical bridges tend to reflect that ambivalence.

The Witness as Camera
Cameras have worn the figurative badge of "witness" for a very long time; by contrast, human, flesh-and-blood legal witnesses are relatively rarely characterized as cameras. The reversal does, however, make a certain kind of sense. Logomorphist extraordinary, the human witness

performs the function, from the perspective of legal process, of a knowledge sponge: a container with duration in time and extent in space, capable of absorbing events and information as they occur and subsequently made available to be wrung out in the official and public act of testifying.[1] There is, of course, a temporal disjunction between the act of witnessing (i.e., coming into possession of knowledge) and the act of bearing witness (i.e., making that knowledge available). The logic of the courtroom—or, perhaps, the metaphysics of the courtroom—ritually dissolves that temporal disjunction, in large part through the agency of probabilistic reasoning. *Credibility* in a witness combined with *plausibility* in a narrative yields *veracity*, a condition where event and narrative enter into a relationship of functional, effective identity.

In *Eyewitness Testimony*, Elizabeth Loftus offers an extensive study of the dominance of what I am calling the "sponge" model of the witness and a penetrating critique of its flaws. She begins by sketching out a three-stage process: "During the first stage—acquisition—an event is perceived and information about it is initially stored in memory. In the second stage—retention—information is resident in memory. In the final stage—retrieval—memory is searched and pertinent information is retrieved and communicated."[2] The balance of the book is devoted largely to the project of explaining and documenting the fact that information can undergo change in *any* of these three phases. Loftus's study includes research on the difficulties of cross-racial identification, the effects of the wording of questions on memory ("About how fast were the cars going when they ['hit' vs. 'smashed into'] each other?"),[3] the phenomenon of "weapon focus," and many other factors that contravene the sponge theory of the witness but are generally overlooked by intuition and professionalism alike. For Loftus, the efficacy of the human witness as replicator of events is highly overrated—implicitly by the legal system and explicitly by many practitioners and lay people. That overestimation consists of, or evaluates to, an adherence to the belief in the purity of the three-phase journey by which the witnessed event reaches the courtroom.

We need neither insist too much nor dwell too long on the exactness of the fit to remark that film travels a congruent three-phase path, taking the three phases, roughly, as filming (acquisition), postproduction (retention), and projection (retrieval). Less important here than the question of how closely we wish to analogize the three phases themselves is the point that film offers itself for, operates by, and even cultivates *the same mistake* as that made in the case of the human witness: namely, that there exists the possibility of pure replication—in fact, pure phenomenography.[4] In both cases, a disintegrated and transformative process finds itself touted institutionally as purely replicative, and its material trace held to that criterion.

Various institutional and systemic aspects of both courtroom and movie theater procedure seize on and nourish any embryonic evidence assumption that the regimes in question are phenomenographic. In the case of film, this refers largely (if it is still meaningful to speak of this as an isolable factor) to the ostensible automatic veracity of recording technologies based in photographic processes—in short, all the ramifications of the dictum, "The camera never lies." In court, where lying cannot be wished away a priori, the witness is cushioned by the elaborate and solemn trappings of the oath, by the ceremony, and even by the architecture and dress of the occasion. Ritual and the appeal to ethics, in other words, stand in for the technologically determined aura of veracity surrounding film.

In both cases, then, certain conditions of history and acculturation tend toward the phenomenographic fallacy. Indeed, that fallacy has prevailed: the intuitive or aesthetically compelling likelihood of phenomenography has, it seems, issued into its triumphant cultural achievement—post hoc, to all appearances, ergo propter hoc. But this apparent connection invites closer scrutiny of the intervening forces, of the nature of the friction that holds the expectation against its fulfillment. That search leads us back to narrative, the fail-safe or guarantor of event-replicative powers. As the sheer desire for phenomenography meets up with its ostensible achievement in institutional contexts, narrative as a material commodity remains highly perceptible, even as narrative as a structuring and first principle disappears into the folds. It therefore appears that film and the legal witness are replicating events *as a result of*, in a manner directly connected to or growing out of, illusionistic technology and the solemnity of courtroom ceremony, oath taking, and discursive allegiance to truth. But whatever happens in the outer reaches of the process, narrative is always there, circulating among public discourses and private mental representations, holding them together like the sturdy inner tube of a more vulnerable tire.[5]

The circuitry connecting, in this manner, representation to truth—or logomorph to phenomenograph—probably appears most clearly in the case of film. However, following Bennett and Feldman, and leaning on Loftus, we can trace it in the case of the human witness as well. A more abstract description of the path catches up the witness's journey in its language: for example, *from* the achievement of a viable, probabilistic verbal narrative version *to* the accreditation of the narrating instrument (film, witness) as a purely replicative device of event-retrieval. In these terms, we evoke the phenomenographical mythology of both witness and cinema.

This, I believe, is the mutual function of the centralizing of narrative in the bids for phenomenographical status of both regimes—a centralizing celebrated in one, kept quiet in the other. The act of event replication is an apparently likely result of certain preconditions of each process *and* the final purported accomplishment of each. Holding these two registers together, however, is the antiphenomenographical narrative imperative, differently configured but equally in the ascendance. The speech of the witness and the sensory data of the film behave as optional, nonnecessary, occasional representations of something that might have been represented otherwise—represented more correctly, at greater length, more briefly, less well, more plausibly. In both cases, the discursive instrument (witness, film) earns the title of phenomenographer in a victory gained on the battlefield of narrative form. Thus, in a system that generates and revels in multiple narrative representations produced by an agency with compelling prior qualifications as phenomenographer, the determination that a given term may stand in for the event *issues from* a finding of correctly crafted, topically sound narrative and *results in* the conferral of phenomenographic status.

And the glue is clearly stronger than the material. This is where narrativity meets up with the tenacity of the realist longing—something, in fact, beyond realism. The representation—the narrative utterance, version, or term—is welded to its referent with the highly adhesive medium of a separately negotiated credibility and then reinvested in the basic process of the institution. This is a greater friction, and a more durable bond, than any arising out of the actual nature of either cinematography or verbal discourse.

The courtroom witness functions in the capacity of synoptist, but so do other players in the courtroom: lawyers (in their addresses to the jury and the court, or in introducing evidence), defendants, unexpected confessors, and so forth. Courtroom participants function as supplicants for or providers of narrative, and any given individual can perform both roles at different times. Within the terms of this flux and counterflux, it is in general the position of provider of narrative that may be designated by the term "synoptist"—the witness being the most fully developed but not the only example.

The analogy with film holds, even in these broader terms, in that the narrative cinema similarly beats to the pulse of the *supplication for* and *dispensation of* narrative. Both the courtroom and the cinema play host to this transaction, such that a synoptist or a synoptic instrument of narrative production may aspire to (and be granted) the status of phenomenographer. But there is a paradox here: these operations take place within arenas of firmly entrenched and extensive narrative activity, abundantly productive of multiple, contingent, mutable, conflicting, and exchangeable versions. The myth of phenomenography, in other words, has to survive—and does survive—in contexts that, examined obliquely, we might rather expect to aid in its debunking. Any search for a storehouse of narrative uncertainty and relativity need go no further than the legal system or the cinema. Yet those institutions almost unswervingly relativize their own relativity against an ostensibly unassailable phenomenographic premise.

Interestingly, the examination of the circuitry of event, logomorph, and phenomenograph takes us back to Loftus—who, in passing, uses videography as a counterexample to the relativity and nonphenomenographic nature of the legal witness: "When we experience an important event, we do not simply record that event in memory as a videotape recorder would."[6] My point, of course, is that a videotape recorder—or a film camera—is also incapable of the pure, linear phenomenography for which it so often receives credit and which Loftus convincingly explores and exposes in the case of the human witness.

Detection, Film, and Language

If the basic trajectory of legal procedure is toward the propositional, the verbal, the containable in language, many legal cases nonetheless begin very far from words and the clean contours of verbal synopsis. Detective procedure can play an important role in the journey from the heterogeneity of the event to the crucible of the courtroom, where logos is ceremonially stripped of its extraverbal encrustations.[7]

In *The Psychology of Eyewitness Testimony*, A. Daniel Yarmey lays out schematically the course of criminal legal process. In commenting on the elements represented, Yarmey emphasizes the transformation of miscellaneous data into evidence and evidence into facts. Among other things, he points out that legal "facts" and intuitive "facts"— including, for instance, a crime victim's personal convictions about "what happened"—are two different things: "The layperson often makes the erroneous assumption that his or her 'facts' will automatically be accepted as the truth by the judge or jury. We often act as if facts exist separate from us as individuals in some sort of self-evident, ideal form which can be copied and given to another person."[8] Once the rules of evidence have been brought to bear, however, the resultant legal facts have, or behave as if they have, precisely the characteristics of resilience and repeatability that, as Yarmey suggests, the law regards as specious in the case of facts of the nonlegal order.

As a kind of roadmap to his discussion of the topic, Yarmey uses a simple left-to-right flow chart to identify the various phases in the life cycle of a criminal case, from "Crime Committed" through police investigation, trial, judicial determination of facts, jury deliberation, and "Decision."[9] The right side of the chart illustrates the ultimate distillation into language: the assignment of the verdict, the single word. The left side bears on our current topic, investigation and detection. Yarmey discusses several aspects of detective work, placing both scientific method and phenomenological description among its components. He builds a preliminary (i.e., precourtroom) link between the heterogeneity of the space and time of the crime and the formulation of a solution: "Once the nature of the crime is known, the task of discovering, applying, fitting, modifying, and finally of rejecting or accepting potential solutions begins. . . . The facts discovered by the investigator are constantly organized and reorganized in an attempt to discover any logical patterns. At the same time, the investigator may construct hypotheses, or tentative post hoc solutions."[10]

This description of detective work (though not the only facet Yarmey describes) will serve as our bridge to the world of film theory. In fact, this particular bridge takes us back to David Bordwell and his Constructivist/hypothesis-framing take on the cognition of film: "In watching a representational film, we draw on schemata derived from our transactions with the everyday world, with other artworks, and with other films. On the basis of these schemata, we make assumptions, erect expectations, and confirm or disconfirm hypotheses. Everything from recognizing objects and understanding dialogue to comprehending the film's overall story utilizes previous knowledge."[11]

At this stage, any link between detective work as sketched out by Yarmey and spectatorial work as sketched out by Bordwell[12] is somewhat subterranean. The link may, indeed, consist of no more than the family resemblance between Bordwell's Constructivist approach and scientific method (in general and as reflected in Yarmey's description of detection in particular). Bordwell does, however, join up explicitly with the detective metaphor in his subsequent elaborations, relying heavily on detective films as key texts and making pointed comparisons between detective characters and the spectator. In his extended discussion of *Rear Window*, he suggests that "the process whereby Jeff pursues the mystery displays quite beautifully the activity of the film spectator."[13] He also analyzes the characters' activities in terms that directly echo the theoretical language he has already introduced in connection with spectatorship: "Now [Jeff] can apply a very loose procedural schema. . . . The next morning, he possesses only the roughest hypothesis. . . . That evening there is a pitched battle of mutually exclusive hypotheses."[14]

Bordwell discusses detective films in the context of the notion of syuzhet and fabula. Any one fabula, Bordwell explains, may be expressed in any number of syuzhets, and it is characteristic of the detective genre that key data of the fabula (who did it? what happened?) are obscured rather than revealed by the syuzhet: "The fundamental narrational characteristic of the detective tale is that the syuzhet withholds crucial events occurring in the 'crime' portion of the fabula. The syuzhet may conceal the motive, or the planning, or the commission of the crime. . . . [The] syuzhet is principally structured by the progress of the detective's investigation."[15]

Bordwell's discussion of detective films in general, and his detailed analyses of several in particular, once again closely ties the spectator's activity in with that of the characters, especially the detective. It would be reductive to suggest that he "equates" spectator and character; he does, however, explore the detective/spectator analogy in several respects and at several levels.

The missing piece of the picture, at this stage, is Bordwell's position on the role of language in the cognition of narrative cinema. I have suggested that, in complex and sometimes ironic ways, film and law share a drive toward the verbal—film, as a precondition of its narrativity; law, as a means of making the outside world available to the system. Detective work, moreover, contributes to this process in the case of law.

Bordwell has privileged the detective, and the detective genre, as being kindred to the filmic spectator. By pure analogical reasoning, therefore, we might expect to find him following up his use of the detective metaphor with a profession of belief in language as the cognitive, or at least metaphorical, key to filmic spectatorship.

As we have seen, however, Bordwell positions himself in the clearest possible terms as an *opponent* of the many branches of film theory that have approached filmic cognition in the context of language, verbal activity, and/or linguistic structure. This putting aside of language-centered paradigms generates internal tensions. The "loaf of bread" argument, for example, hardly sounds like the writings of someone out to *reject* the film/language connection. Here, again, is the relevant passage: "Comprehending a narrative requires assigning it some coherence. At a local level, the viewer must grasp character relations, lines of dialogue, relations between shots, and so on. More broadly, the viewer must test the narrative information for consistency: does it hang together in a way we can identify? For instance, does a series of gestures, words, and manipulations of objects add up to the action sequence we know as 'buying a loaf of bread'?"[16]

As I have already suggested, this passage might assist in making the case *for* the idea that the cognition of film has a great deal to do with the assignment of conscious, or at least potentially conscious, verbal labels to sensory data—that is, for precisely the organization of the world by the subject through language that Bordwell explicitly rejects. The additional and salient point here is that in Bordwell's case we see a theorist of narrative film attempting two things: first, to escape the pull of language as the center of theory; and second, to explore the metaphor of the detective, and the conventions of the detective genre, as a means of explicating the processes of the cognition of filmic narrative. These do not succeed equally, nor do they coexist in peace. In a sense, this might have been predicted from what we have already seen of law and film and the role of language. It is the detective's job to hasten the journey toward the word, to begin to prepare the miscellany of the physical, social world for its day in court, for its ritual transformation into facts. "Buying a loaf of bread" is a fact, a proposition, up to which any number of filmic miscellanies might equally have led. Bordwell's example implies (though he wants to deny it) that what ties different versions of an event together is their common tethering to similar verbal constructs—that two or three or four films in which someone buys a loaf of bread are about the same thing *because* we assign them to the same verbal, factual category.[17] The spectator-as-detective metaphor suggests, in my view, a close connection between filmic cognition and natural language, and Bordwell's attempt to have the metaphor without that connection consequently bears a considerable strain.[18]

Notes

1. I am not suggesting that anyone with a grasp of the nature of human testimony actually believes in this idealized model; rather, the system is based on this model, however unbelievable it may be.

2. Elizabeth Loftus, *Eyewitness Testimony* (Cambridge, Mass.: Harvard University Press, 1979), xii.

3. Ibid., 77.

4. I hope I may be allowed this neologism, for which I cannot claim even as tenuous a pedigree as for "logomorph." "Phenomenography" seems to me to encapsulate exactly the status accorded to filmic representations and, in some respects, to credible legal testimony. Furthermore, it bypasses the circuitry of logomorphism—that is, the passage of such representation and testimony through a phase, or layer, of linguistic or propositional form. Since I believe that circuitry to be always involved, I intend the term "phenomenography" to refer to an ideal that is probably never actually attained.

5. If not, then—to point in a couple of directions in which I will not go any farther—on what basis may a false witness be believed, or, for that matter, an animated film even comprehended?

6. Loftus, 21.

7. For a more-empirical, less-theoretical take on the relation between criminal investigation and the courtroom, see Peter W. Greenwood, Jan M. Chaiken, and Joan Petersilia, *The Criminal Investigation Process* (Lexington, Mass.: D. C. Heath, 1977).

8. A. Daniel Yarmey, *The Psychology of Eyewitness Testimony* (New York: Free Press, 1979), 27.

9. Ibid., 24 (fig. 2.1).

10. Ibid., 27.

11. David Bordwell, *Narration in the Fiction Film* (Madison: University of Wisconsin Press, 1985), 32–33.

12. Spectatorship is work for Bordwell: "In opposition to all passive notions of spectatorship, then, we should consider film viewing a complicated, even skilled, activity" (ibid., 33).

13. Ibid., 41.

14. Ibid., 41–42.

15. Ibid., 66.

16. Ibid., 34.

17. For an extended discussion of the relation between narrative utterances and their referent events, see David Alan Black, "Narrative Film and the Synoptic Tendency" (Ph.D. diss., New York University, 1988).

18. I cannot leave this topic without quoting a passage from a recent work on criminal investigation that offers an intriguing glimpse of the flow of influence in the less predictable of the possible directions: "Some current investigative practices appear mainly as a means to preserve a media-like image or to give a victim the kind of services he expects largely because of that image. That is, fingerprint dusting, mug shot showing, or questioning witnesses are often done without any hope of developing leads, but simply for public relations" (Greenwood et al., 9).

6

Legal Scholarship Looks at Film

Opening Argument

Legal scholars and writers on law-related topics mention film a lot. In fact, a Lexis/Nexis search on the word "film" yielded so many results (over 4,000) that the software refused to allow me to download the list. Much of this material is not of interest here (matters pertaining to intellectual property in the visual arts; the use of "day-in-the-life" films in the courtroom; commentary on various lawsuits involving film companies; and so forth). The focus here will be on a particular body of work, namely, academic essays published in law reviews, law journals, and interdisciplinary ("Law and . . .") journals pertaining to film.

The thesis of this chapter is that, although legal scholars have in fact written a fair amount about film, there is still something left to say about the subject of law in film, specifically from the point of view of film studies and specifically from the perspectives outlined so far in this book. This chapter is based on an examination of about fifteen years of academic legal scholarship that focuses on film and will include comments on interdisciplinary study in the cases of both law and film—that is, how they differ, what they have in common, and how consideration of interdisciplinary work can help us position the current project. Legal scholars have written about film and filmic narrative; nonetheless, for reasons arguably having to do with both the agenda of such work and its relative lack of contact with the field of film studies, an examination of it reveals, among other things, that an intervention from film studies is probably a good idea. If nothing else, it may serve to bring a number of essays about film into the view of film scholars who might otherwise not have encountered them.

The context for this exploration will be, primarily, the law-and-literature movement of the last twenty or so years. As we will see, this movement has provided a starting point—sometimes an explicit one, sometimes simply an intellectual environment—for a substantial, though not enormous, amount of legal scholarship on film. The movement itself *is* enormous and rather sprawling; accordingly, my goal here is not to chronicle it thoroughly but to understand it to the extent that it helps to make sense of the law-and-film work under consideration. As we move from the broadest level (interdisciplinary trends in legal scholarship), through the intermediate (the law-and-literature movement), to the most circumscribed (legal scholarship's treatment of film), I will offer general comments as well as some extended remarks on particularly important and/or representative essays.

The law-and-literature movement operates, and is frequently discussed, in the yet wider context of a growing trend in interdisciplinary scholarship within legal academia. It is worth looking initially at that trend in general, not only to make sense of the law-and-literature movement, but also because the law-and-film work to be considered here should not be narrowly understood as a tendril or subset of law-and-literature but also, in its own right, as another "law-and- . . ." exercise.

Importantly, a great deal of legal scholarship on film serves a pedagogical purpose. It tends to be about curricula and teaching (including reflections on what has happened in the classroom when films have been used as objects of study, as well as ideas about how to use them) rather than about practicing law. Then again, legal pedagogy is always in some sense "about" practicing law. This is a connection I will have occasion to explore later in more depth.

Law and Literature: A Layperson's Overview

In the course of an evaluative look at the law-and-literature movement (and many of that movement's texts are, in fact, evaluative looks), C. R. B. Dunlop surveys the state of interdisciplinary work in law and explains the nature and extent of some of the controversies involved. The law-and-literature movement, as Dunlop explains, comes out of—and should be seen as part of—an increasingly interdisciplinary expansion in the scope of legal scholarship and pedagogy and a calling into question of the very idea of law as a self-contained, self-sufficient academic field. "The vision of law as an autonomous discipline has increasingly come under attack during the past 25 years. . . . Traditional legal education has been condemned for its insularity and its 'limits of breadth, depth, and imagination,' limits that have led legal researchers and teachers to 'fail to consider the intellectual and political world outside the law schools.'" The result has been change: curricular change, in the direction of interdisciplinary expansion, and even attempts "to redefine the nature of law itself."[1]

To make sense of the increasingly important role of a number of "law and . . ." subdisciplines, Dunlop makes a distinction between research *in* law and research *about* law. The former harmonizes with the more traditional structure of legal education, while the latter opens the door to the many "and's," including literature: "Research *in* law often (perhaps always) consists of doctrinal analysis of legal texts such as cases or statutes. . . . [It] tends not to involve empirical study of the actual workings of the legal order or of its economic or social consequences. It becomes the study of a limited set of texts rather than an examination of the actual workings of legal institutions. . . . [It] usually does not cross disciplinary boundaries. . . . It apparently has a coherence and an autonomy enabling one to call it a discipline."[2] By contrast, research *about* law allows law to be discussed

> as an historical phenomenon, as a cultural, philosophical, or political idea, or as an institution having social, political, or economic consequences that can be examined empirically. Law can be seen as the kind of discourse that can be probed for its use of metaphor or myth. It can be read as a story. . . . research *about* law seems almost always to involve disciplines other than law. One is driven to examine history, the social sciences, cultural studies, philosophy, and literature to carry out the project.[3]

Dunlop's own views on the merits of the two approaches are made clear, particularly when he narrows the focus from the general terms of the in/about distinction to the particular case of the relevance to the law of the study of literature:

> Legal scholarship can and should include studies of works of literature dealing with law. Fiction may not be particularly helpful as a way to learn legal rules or history, but it can tell us much *about* law, defined broadly to mean the legal order. . . . The assumption of traditional legal education, that law is a technical and insular matter grasped entirely or largely on its own, has been replaced by the belief that it is inextricably bound up with politics,

morality, culture, and life. . . . The center of legal scholarship will always be law, but scholars should approach it as a part of a broader civilization.[4]

This is not to say that the traditional doctrinal analysis approach and the more inclusive one are mutually exclusive, but rather that at least some scholarship should deal with "law-and- . . ." subject matter.

If the law-and-literature movement can be understood, in its origins, as part of the right half of the "research in/research about" pair, the movement itself has also been understood as falling into two parts: "law-*in*-literature" and "law-*as*-literature." "'Law *in* literature' is, as the name suggests, the study of representations of the legal order in fiction, usually novels and plays. Courses on the subject require students to read several books in which the law plays a significant role. . . . [In 'law *as* literature'] the focus is on law, not literature. Law *as* literature draws insights from literary criticism and theory to assist in the reading and interpretation of legal texts, particularly judicial decisions."[5]

We might add, here, other threads that more or less, or intermittently, identify themselves with the movement, particularly studies of legal storytelling and explorations of law in the context of narrative. These identifying terms function more as centers of gravity than as absolute markers of intellectual territory; in practice, there is a lot of overlap among them. What unites them is an embrace of both extralegal fictional texts, as paradigms or even parables of the law, and/or the interpretation of legal texts (including legal interpretive texts) as literary or narrative. This has, of course, tremendous implications across the board. Whether it is a matter of taking fictional representations seriously as sources of ideas about the law or of treating legal discourses as stories (thereby putting them in the same boat as fictional discourses, at least for purposes of understanding their narrative strategies and economies of persuasion), all of these closely related approaches have the effect of taking the law down a notch, in terms of its authority and the putative absolute meaning of its texts.

Dunlop sketches out the controversies that have accompanied this shift in legal pedagogy and scholarship. I will return to some of these later in the course of discussing the relation and relevance of the movement to the study of film. Debate has raged on both the merits of the case—that is, the question of whether studying literature is an appropriate part of legal scholarship at all—and the logistics—that is, whether there is, in practical terms, adequate space and time in the course of a basic legal education to take courses in which one reads novels instead of statutes. Whatever the controversies, law and litera-ture has certainly taken hold in law school curricula and academic publications; while not a replacement for traditional legal education, it now fully exists within or alongside it.

The increasingly interdisciplinary nature of legal scholarship is, of course, part of a yet broader trend in academic discourse generally. As Dunlop suggests, "traditional law courses must draw from other disci-plines; in the present intellectual climate, it would be hard not to do so."[6] This intellectual climate is, for example, the climate in which film studies has turned prolifically to literary theory, not to mention economics, sociology, ethnography, and psychoanalysis. We may now confidently anticipate seeing the same familiar names (Derrida, Barthes, Foucault, Hayden White, etc.) in the footnotes of essays in many fields. As we will see, however, this inclusive approach has very different meanings for different fields, and certainly for law and film.

The search for the perfect connector between "law" and "literature" may be a futile one, but we might summarize the whole enterprise as involving the construction or understanding of law *through* literature. Much of the work clustering around this movement undertakes to use literature and/or literary theory to gain purchase on matters of legal pedagogy, philosophy, and practice. Novels and short stories are intro-duced because—in the opinion of their curricular sponsors—they make the road to professionalism more complete and more meaningful. Ideas from literary theory are explored because they offer an alternative, per-haps even a corrective, to some of the traditionally dominant modes of interpretation of legal texts. Legal discourses—statutes, judicial opin-ions, courtroom arguments—are described and analyzed as storytelling or narrative and thereby strung onto the same strand as the extralegal cultural practices of which they are a part. The point, institutionally, is not to replace LL.B.'s with joint degrees in law and literature but to get from the world of literature what we can by way of help toward a legal education. The point, intellectually, is not to pursue literary studies as an end in itself but, still operating in the interests of a basically tradi-tional professional training, to use literature and literary theory as tools for gaining access to otherwise invisible or recalcitrant aspects of law.

Marijane Camilleri's 1990 article "Lessons in Law from Literature: A Look at the Movement and a Peer at Her Jury" may serve as a repre-sentative example of work in law and literature.[7] Like many essays emerging from this approach, Camilleri's includes reflections on the movement itself (indeed, one wonders whether the movement ever went through any kind of innocent, non-self-evaluative phase): "The law and literature movement proposes that the science of textual interpretation has interdisciplinary utility and that it is worthwhile to explore the congruous elements of literary and legal hermeneutics because the former is likely to illuminate the latter."[8] She strongly supports the movement and includes, by way of illustrating its strengths, an exegetical commentary on the 1917 short story "A Jury of Her Peers" by Susan Glaspell. Toward the beginning of her essay, Camilleri frames some of the concerns and defenses of the movement, taking, perhaps, a somewhat sanguine view of the usefulness of the law-and-literature approach:

> To many unacquainted with the movement, law and literature seem almost mutually exclusive enterprises. Certainly, a legal work and a literary work are at once distinguishable. . . . Exponents of the [law-and-literature] movement utilize the very qualities of literature, such as its experiential character, that cause skeptics to challenge the wisdom of incorporating literature into the study of law. . . . The diversity of viewpoints on the role of literature in the practice and study of law attests to the richness of literature as a source for legal discussion. . . .[9]

Camilleri proceeds to explore those respects in which literature, as a cultural and aesthetic practice, has, in its difference from law (and the differences between its texts and legal texts), something to offer legal thinking and scholarship. In particular, she favors it over other "law-and- . . ." approaches:

> The value of law lies not in abstractions, but in its capacity to respond to extrinsic realities. The law and literature movement reveals a frustration with the narrow language of the social sciences and analytic philosophy—disciplines which tend to lead us further away from the extrinsic realities and deeper into the abstract. While these disciplines will always remain highly useful to law, they do not provide a direct encounter with the concrete experience of daily living which literature uniquely achieves, particularly through its narrative form.[10]

In particular, Camilleri argues, "when literature exposes the realities of an historically underrepresented or unrepresented class of persons, such as women, minorities, or the handicapped, the importance of reading literature for lawyers becomes particularly acute. Literature vividly communicates the voices of these classes, which traditionally have been muffled or co-opted by the legal system."[11] Literature, in other words, has the potential to help the legal scholar—and the lawyer— achieve escape velocity from a system of representation and interpretation that cannot point or see beyond a restricted set of histories and assumptions. (Again, Camilleri's argument has a somewhat optimistic tone. If, indeed, "literature can prepare the lawyer to respond to diverse perspectives, such as those of feminists, by stimulating open dialogue about where the law is unjust,"[12] we nonetheless might question how often this is likely to happen in so straightforward a manner and, if exposure to narratives of injustice were all that were required to liberalize antifeminists, why it had not happened already.)

Camilleri pursues her argument by examining ways in which legal scholarship can borrow, and has borrowed, from literary-theoretical techniques, here taking the "law-*as*-literature" fork in the road, at least for the time being. She comments on a number of familiar angles of revision and attack common to much mid- to late-twentieth-century literary criticism (her sections include "The Liberation of the Text from the Author," "The Inversion of the Hierarchies," and "An Application of the Deconstructionist Technique to Law"). In each case, she is concerned to demonstrate that literary theory has something to contribute to legal scholarship—not that legal texts are either formally or functionally identical to literary texts, but that literary theory has (unlike traditional modes of legal interpretation) given itself the scope to troubleshoot the nature of texts in ways from which legal scholarship now has something to learn.

Camilleri shifts from a general discussion of the law-and-literature movement and its critics to an example of the approach in action. (This mixing of levels of theory and application is fairly typical of essays in this field.) Turning to her case study, the short story "A Jury of Her Peers" by Susan Glaspell, Camilleri performs first "A Literary Interpretation of the Story" and then "A Legal Application of the Story," in which she suggests that the themes and concerns raised in the course of the story might profitably be explored in law school discussions.

Interestingly, Camilleri's "literary interpretation" is surprisingly deterministic, giving very little attention to issues such as immanency of meaning, authorial intention, and reader response. The interpretation—and it is noteworthy that she has called it an interpretation rather than a deconstruction—revolves around the digging out of metaphors and symbols:

> The masculine sounding "Dickson County" is a metaphor for the pervading masculine legal culture. Martha's abrupt departure from her "ordinary" routine, leaving the bread she was making unfinished, with "half the flour sifted and half unsifted," signals the subtle, but drastic break with the past and the radical transformation of the women of Dickson County that is about to occur. The "half sifted," "half unsifted" flour is a metaphor for both the arrested self-development of the women under the established law and culture, and the deficient nature of the established law and culture itself.[13]

Certainly, there is nothing particularly radical about this interpretation, either in its methodology (providing a running gloss on metaphors) or in its implied position on the nature of literature (that it is of determined meaning). Camilleri takes the ideal, implied reader at face value, though she does so in the service of making a point about the possibility of using literature in a legal context. At a moment when the protagonist

> subconsciously experiences the appalling inequity of her realization that the law is perniciously intrusive and debilitating to women . . . [the] reader, empathizing with Mrs. Hale, temporarily assumes her feminine perspective. As a result, the story interacts with the reader in a profoundly unique way, compelling the reader's subordination of any personal parochial perspective or bias and promoting the reader's exploration of the perspective of the protagonist.[14]

My purpose in traversing Camilleri's essay is not to berate her for literary-theoretical nonencyclopedism, nor to judge her commentary against some imaginary yardstick of an acceptable degree of reader relativity and textual indeterminacy (though I must say that I hit a snag at the claim that this story was "profoundly unique" in its ability to determine reader response). Rather, my point is that the law-and-literature approach, though it *may* involve tremendous degrees of communion with trends in literary theory, does not necessarily or always do so. At the same time, this may or may not actually matter. Camilleri is pursuing a literary interpretation because doing so opens the door to discussions, *by people for whom it might make a difference*, to important issues.

This point is carried through in the essay's next section, "A Legal Application of the Story," in which Camilleri draws certain conclusions and starting points for legal reflection—and action—from the story. Specifically, she draws attention to the issue of *inclusion*—that is, inclusion in the legal system of groups traditionally excluded or marginalized. She makes a direct connection between this issue and the story:

> "A Jury of Her Peers" is a reflection on the idea that institutions established by men and predominantly for men, such as the law, are deficient and even brutish without the feminine perspective. . . . [The story] provided a non-violent and articulate register of women's cry for inclusion and could have penetrated the walls of law schools, complementing a technical course on criminal procedure, and inviting prospective legal representatives to explore rationally the rights of women at a time when women, themselves, were not likely to be found in law school.[15]

This particular story, in other words, illustrates the kind of literature that might, by its inclusion in the law school curriculum (and through attention paid by legal scholars), expand the horizons of legal education to include urgent issues that otherwise would not adequately surface. Then again, it might not. A certain amount of Camilleri's exegesis of metaphors, and even her recourse to such theoretical points of reference as deconstruction, seems to gain relatively little new purchase on the question of the relevance of law to literature. For instance, where she discusses the matter of a feminist rethinking of rape statutes and characterizes that rethinking as "deconstructionist," the arguments carry a great deal of weight, while their categorization as deconstructive floats unengaged around them—that is, deconstruction operates as an after-the-fact label applied to an already challenging and robust argument.

In any case, Camilleri's article provides a representative and lucid point of entry to the law-and-literature realm. Much of legal writing about film has identified itself, in one way or another, with legal writing on literature; and it is to legal writing about film that I now turn.

Law and/as/in Film: A Critical Survey of Selected Essays

> There may be bookish souls who stay confined within the four corners of their constitutional texts and do not get to the movies very often.[16]

It would be an oversimplification to claim a law-and-literature pedigree for every academic legal article about film. The articles in question do not make up that coherent a body of work but, rather, are chiefly connected by their mutual attention to film. In any case, as we shall see, the way legal scholarship handles film has some close connections with the way it handles literature—and some extremely telling divergences.

One of the issues I will comment on toward the end of this examination is the extent to which the essays under consideration do or do not represent substantial work in the area of film studies. While this is not a simple question, and perhaps one that will never admit of anything but subjective reasoning, I would like to start with an essay that strikes me as being at the upper end, by this criterion. The article in question is "Taking Exception to Six Decades on Film: A Social History of Women Lawyers in Popular Culture, 1930 to 1990" by Ric Sheffield.[17]

Sheffield traces the history of the representation of women lawyers in film and television, offering the results of very detailed research. Along the way, he makes a series of connections between the world on the screen and the real world of the legal profession; moreover, these connections vary interestingly in type and are by no means all of the familiar "Is it accurate?" variety. Examples of the kinds of connections he draws are: statistics about women lawyers in the workplace and their representation in film (e.g., the fact that while "there were an estimated 10,000 African-American women practicing law in this country . . . there has been only one African-American actress regularly cast as a featured attorney on prime-time television"[18]); biographical background on creative personnel (e.g., the fact that Faith Baldwin, author of *Portia on Trial*, first encountered a woman lawyer in the context of her father's activities as an attorney and was "dismayed"[19]); and interaction between the legal profession and the film industry in connection with promotion and reception of films (e.g., the filing of a complaint about *Portia* by the Los Angeles Bar Association;[20] the arrangement of special screenings of and distribution of promotional materials on *Disbarred* to law schools;[21] studio executives' attempts to palm actress Gail Patrick off as a law student[22]).

In fact, perhaps the weakest link in the chain—that is, the least robustly documented and least confidently asserted area of influence and connection—is the matter of the influence of representations of women lawyers on the public and the profession. This is, of course, virtually impossible to document meaningfully. Sheffield resorts—quite responsibly—to noticeably tenuous language, as the following passage from his conclusion suggests:

It is difficult to believe that media depictions of women lawyers have not influenced real world expectations of the appropriate dress, demeanor, and style of women engaged in the legal profession. While it may be argued that such depictions merely reflect the inhospitable realities confronting women lawyers in what many continue to call a male profession, it is undeniable that the mere presentation of such attitudes and behavior may work to reinforce them for both victims and victimizers. Many women lawyers likely are influenced by the dramatization of negative consequences for certain behaviors and thereby seek to avoid them altogether. This may explain the prevalence of what some have referred to as "androgynous" female attorneys.[23]

The speculative tone of this passage is understandable, though striking when placed next to some of the extremely detailed documentation that characterizes much of the rest of the essay. It happens that this essay, including the speculative parts (which are more convincing in their speculations than a lot of other speculative writings), has considerable weight as film historical scholarship and would certainly not attract negative attention, or seem out of place, in a film studies journal. What is particularly interesting, in this connection, is that the essay is *not* in a film studies journal but in a law journal. Its primary identity is as an essay in legal studies, though it may also be described as an example of responsible and substantial film scholarship that functions as something else—and *is* something else.

Indeed, the effective category of the scholarship is in large part determined by the audience: legal scholarship is that which is read by readers of legal journals, who are mostly academic lawyers. This does not mean that film scholars cannot read it, but, playing the percentages, it is reasonable to speculate that a lot of them do not. There is a defining connection between the audience and the type of scholarship involved.

Sheffield's article is actually fairly exceptional in its congruence with film studies. Many legal articles about film are more clearly, or perhaps more exclusively, exercises in legal scholarship and pedagogy. In this particular respect, they resemble Camilleri's essay discussed earlier. An example of this is Aviam Soifer's article "Complacency and Constitutional Law," which is basically about the 1980 Supreme Court case *City of Mobile v. Bolden,* a case that revolves around the issue of discriminatory election districting:

In *Bolden*, the Court rejects a claim by black citizens that they are denied their "constitutionally protected right to participate in elections on an equal basis with other citizens in the jurisdiction." . . . The essential claim in *Bolden* is that the racially polarized bloc voting in Mobile, exacerbated by several elements of the [still-enforced] 1911 election format, freezes black citizens out of the political community. This is compounded by the fact, as found by the lower courts, that Mobile is unresponsive to the claims of black citizens for municipal services, employment, and similar ordinary governmental functions.[24]

There are, in other words, significant legal and social issues at stake in this case. In the second part of the article, Soifer analyzes—and excoriates—the Supreme Court's opinion, which found for the city, by identifying and setting forth three pernicious aspects of it: "The Ahistorical Stance," "The Neutral Pose," and "The Unexplained Happy Ending." Soifer argues that Justice Potter Stewart's opinion is rooted in an ahistorical and preposterous syllogism:

1. In 1911, Mobile enacted an at-large voting pattern, which was part of a nationwide campaign against corruption in city government. . . .
2. In 1911, blacks did not vote in Alabama. [Therefore the] 1911 voting reform could not have been intended to discriminate on the basis of race.[25]

The neutral pose manifests itself in a tendency by the Court "to view itself as something of a benignly neglectful neutral functionary, high above the real life battle. . . . In *Bolden* . . . enthusiastic deference to the institutional status quo is combined with an unwillingness to contemplate past wrongs. The neutrality which results rests on policy rather than on history."[26] "The Unexplained Happy Ending," in this case, is something the Court avoids, because it finds it easier to "explain" a ruling that perpetuates discrimination:

The Court in *Bolden* is scrupulous to avoid an ending which lacks a fully developed theoretical explanation. Fearful of the slippery slope once the notion of political claims by minority groups is loosed on the constitutional landscape, the plurality mischaracterizes Justice Marshall's dissent as a plea for "a constitutional guarantee of proportional representation." In the absence of a full-blown theory akin to the elusive and mythical neutral principle, a majority of the Court equates blacks with all other potential group claimants for purposes of constitutional analysis of their claim to political equality.[27]

Soifer's dissection of the *Bolden* decision is refined, direct, and un-compromising. As for the relevance of film, it consists in Soifer's hav-ing derived the three themes with which he analyzes *Bolden* from an initial analysis of *Casablanca.* The article begins:

> We yearn for blind and disembodied Justice. Yet we also expect and qui-etly hope that in the end, in a vital case, a great Justice will let the mask slip just a bit. We expect the Court to be tough and neutral and above the fray—but we also want it to come through in the crunch. In other words, we assign to the court the Bogart role in "Casablanca."
>
> "Casablanca," in fact, illuminates significant issues in contemporary constitution theory. Through its flickering light, it is possible to focus es-sential problems of discrimination and representation.[28]

Soifer proceeds to recount the plot of *Casablanca*, analyzing it with the use of the three themes ("Movie Version") that he later applies to *Bolden* ("Constitutional Version"). The promise of the preposition "through" in the opening sentences is thus fulfilled: this is truly "law through film," an essay in the use of filmic themes and patterns to get a handle on a legal case.

In that respect, it is analogous to Camilleri's use of "A Jury of Her Peers." At the same time, the two essays operate on very different lev-els. Camilleri is more historical and concrete in what she draws from the story; that is, she chooses the story because it was written by a woman at a certain time in women's history and raises questions that are still, unfortunately, extremely relevant. Her project is nonetheless very speculative: she is suggesting what might happen, or what could happen, were such a literary approach to be incorporated into legal pedagogy. Soifer, on the other hand, is less historical about the extrale-gal text he chooses (indeed, if we wanted to, we could point out that his treatment of *Casablanca* is ahistorical and neutral) but more con-crete about its application to law: he uses it, by analogy, to elucidate what is troubling and wrong about a particular legal case that had specific effects on actual people. The overall pattern is thus similar (ex-tralegal text used to provoke or bolster legal argument), but the coefficients of history, theory, and abstraction are differently disposed.

In a sense, Soifer's recourse to *Casablanca* is unnecessary. Even in iso-lation from the film, the damning paraphrase of Stewart's syllogistic rea-soning is extremely succinct and convincing, as is the rest of the analy-sis of the case. This is not to say that the *Casablanca* strategy lacks rhetorical merit; but only that Soifer's demonstration of the ahistoricism, feigned neutrality, and maintenance of the status quo by the Supreme Court could stand, filmless, on its own. The film and the legal case operate in parallel. Although the use of the film certainly evokes the law-and-literature approach, there is no throwing them into the ring together, no mixing of legal and cinematic blood. It is a low-impact borrowing. Moreover, there is no general theorizing about the relevance of film to law, no reflection on the future of the relationship (not even, "I think this is the beginning of a beautiful friendship"). Soifer's use of the film, in other words, is rhetorical and *occasional:* the analogy works *here* and, as implemented by Soifer, actually does clear a nice path to understanding. But there is no extrapolation or generalization of the idea that film might illuminate law, nor any assertion that the term of comparison had to be a film—rather than, say, another case or a novel.

Another interesting variation on the theme is "Last Night While You Prepared for Class I Went to See *Light of Day:* A Film Review and a Message to My First-Year Property Students, Annotated for My Colleagues," a 1989 article by Robert Laurence.[29] Laurence's strategy in the article, "a very distant descendant of some off-the-cuff remarks delivered to a property class a few years ago,"[30] is to identify, describe, and evaluate two films—*Flashdance* and *Light of Day*—and thereafter, having made certain key distinctions, to use the films' titles as predicate adjectives modifying "law" (among other things). "*Flashdance,*" Laurence argues, "is a terrible movie . . . a story utterly devoid of any reality, a story not a minute of which rings true, a story truly of the 1980's, having as much to do with life as Pittsburgh [the movie's setting] has to do with Fantasyland." This "Cinderella in a hardhat" tale "is gratuitously sexy, and in the end pretty boring."[31]

Light of Day, by contrast, rocks:

> This movie has more energy by several orders of magnitude than *Flashdance.* . . . [Lead actress/rock singer] Joan Jett is possessed of more tightly wound dynamism than I have seen on film in some time. . . . *Light of Day* is also everything that *Flashdance* is not in terms of its story line. Cleveland, in this film, is Cleveland, not Broadway. . . . The film does not compromise one inch in its Clevelandness; it sticks to its reality guns. Welders [the main character's profession in *Flashdance*] are not gorgeous. Bosses may be rich and handsome, and they probably even have sex with their employees, but they don't fall in love with them, and they don't take

them away from the steel mill for life in the Porsche lane—not in Cleveland, not in *Light of Day* they don't.[32]

The battle lines are drawn, and they coincide chiefly with the supposed realism/inaccuracy dichotomy between the two films. I will have more—much more—to say later about the entire phenomenon of probabilistic criticism of film. The point here is that Laurence uses this distinction as a means of entering into a discussion addressed to students about the nature of legal thinking and interpretation. He posits a distinction between "*Flashdance* law" and "*Light of Day* law":

> The assignment for today was *In re Sitkin Smelting and Refining*. . . . The case is difficult. . . . The going is slow and you are restive, I can feel it. . . . Even if you don't seek simple answers, you *do* seek answers, not analysis. . . . You want to arrange the law into tidy packets, best for remembering and dispensing. You seek, in other words, the *Flashdance* version of the law. . . . *Sitkin* and I are here to tell you that the real legal world is the *Light of Day* world.[33]

To practice "*Flashdance* law" is to look for easy answers and to filter out, conveniently, anything that resists or complicates. "*Light of Day* law," by contrast, rolls up its sleeves and deals with the fact that things are difficult, contradictory, and contingent. The titles serve as predicates for other nouns, in addition to law: "the addition of estoppel analysis to BFP discussions makes the complete statement of the law rich and complex. . . . the formulation of that statement is a tough, *Light of Day* task." And, "Maybe time was short; maybe the client could only afford a *Flashdance* brief."[34]

As in Soifer's *Casablanca* essay, film provides expedient categories or predicates for the purpose of saying something about law. There is no sustained attempt here at what one would call film scholarship—nor is there any need for it. The films are useful to the extent that they can be abstracted or made to stand for abstractions. Moreover, Laurence's basic argument is in fact detached from the film review part of his article in the sense that even a student who disagreed with his interpretation of the two films might find persuasive his exhortations about the complexity of the law and the need to be willing to confront difficulties head on when working in the legal field. In other words, there is no integral or necessary engagement with film history or the nature of film, but there is a pedagogical agenda.

David Simon Sokolow, team teaching a University of Texas School of Law contracts course with English professor Susan Sage Heinzelman, decided to show *Rashomon* to the class. Several years later he described the experience in "From Kurosawa to (Duncan) Kennedy: The Lessons of *Rashomon* for Current Legal Education."[35] Sokolow introduced *Rashomon* into the classroom to get the students thinking about legal facts. His concern that legal education tends to gloss over complexities and ambiguities is very much along the lines of Laurence's similar reservations. "Law schools," Sokolow argues,

> are typically good at teaching students about theory and bad at teaching them about facts. Using the Socratic method, the professor investigates the reach of a particular rule of law by forcing a student to apply a given rule to a series of hypothetical fact patterns. Students rarely have to elicit facts; the facts are given as part of the hypothetical.... students often ask "What's the rule?" as if knowing "black letter law" will invariably lead to the "right" result.... Casebook authors often make the matter worse by eliminating the few facts a decision may have included. It seems that the first thing professors and law students do is dispose of the facts.[36]

Sokolow also discusses the virtual omnipresence in legal education of "the professional voice": "a manner of communication that removes law professors from the concerns of ordinary people and suggests that lawyers ought to analyze even the most complex emotional situations by applying a host of abstract rules."[37] This voice, as well as the Socratic method in general, isolates the professor from the students, offering a kind of protection to both parties. Legal education ultimately commits itself away from any acknowledgment of or attention to the emotional, affective, and experiential aspects of the law.

These two streams—the concern with enlightening students about the nature of facts and misgivings about the dominance of the professional voice and all it stands for in the classroom—converged, Sokolow writes, in the execution and aftermath of "what I first conceived as a simple pedagogical experiment designed to teach students in my Contracts class about the importance of facts": namely, a screening of *Rashomon*.[38]

> How far can a lawyer "stretch" the facts to buttress a client's case without misrepresenting them? ... How can a lawyer (or anyone else) ever know what the "truth" really was? In fact, one can ask if there's any such thing as "truth" at all. These questions ... are seldom, if ever, addressed in law

school curricula. To remedy this deficiency, we decided to show the students the classic Japanese film *Rashomon*. . . . Our idea was to show students that facts are subject to interpretation.[39]

Sokolow's use of *Rashomon* is, in some respects, not unlike Camilleri's use of "A Jury of Her Peers"; the idea was to raise student consciousness about an area of legal interpretation not otherwise explicitly discussed in the curriculum. He and Heinzelman showed *Rashomon* to the class in three shifts of thirty students each. The biggest surprises for Sokolow involved the reactions of the students in the first group. There was laughter and whispering during the film, at least one openly distraught reaction to the depiction of rape, and general misunderstanding of the professors' intentions in showing the film in the first place: "'So what you're trying to tell us is that we should bend and twist the facts to suit our client's needs.'"[40]

The reactions of the second and third groups evolved toward what Sokolow had expected and intended; essentially, the second group was bored, and the third group actually "had a thoughtful discussion on the very issues we had intended to address from the start."[41] Sokolow attributes this in part to the fact that he said much more about the film before the screening so as to prepare the students for the subject matter and for the unfamiliar idioms of music and acting style.

Sokolow's further reflections on the episode (which took place several years before the writing of the article) are interestingly confessional. Having started out as an attempt to reveal something to the students, the screening became the occasion of a kind of self-revelation for Sokolow:

> At the time, I viewed myself as an innocent victim of the students' misperceptions. By showing *Rashomon*, I had never intended to advocate a theory of moral relativism. . . . What I failed to recognize was that my intention was not the only force at work. I saw what I wanted to in the film—and the experiment—without considering the students' vantage point. . . . In retrospect, I am confounded by my naiveté in assuming that I could teach students anything in a moral and emotional vacuum. Having shown the students how malleable "facts" are, could I really expect them to view facts "objectively" ever again?[42]

The lesson of *Rashomon*, then, doubles back on itself—and on Sokolow. Film, here, engages very closely with legal pedagogy. Sokolow is not the first to notice that the aftermath of screenings of *Rashomon* often involves people arguing over what "really" happened—even what "really" happened in each of the four versions.[43] Having set out to use the film as a point of entry to fairly abstract ideas (truth is relative, representation is a construct, etc.), he is taken aback by the *non*abstractness of the actual transaction with the students: tears, misunderstanding, differences among the three groups. This is a case where the use of a particular film actually engages very closely with issues of legal pedagogy. In that sense, it is very different from Laurence's *Flashdance/Light of Day* discussion. Here, *Rashomon*—the substance of it, the historical fact of three particular screenings—raises questions and generates thought at an unexpectedly large number of levels.

These articles by Soifer, Laurence, and Sokolow exhibit a range of permutation of classroom, film, and pedagogical purpose. One of the recurrent qualities of such writings (and one that I comment on later in more depth) is that, by and large (and, I believe, for reasons having to with the law-and-literature heritage), the focus is on ways in which *film* does what *literature* does. So far, we have seen rather little grappling by legal scholars with the "specifically cinematic"—that is, with non- and/or extraliterary aspects of film. With the possible exception of *Rashomon*, the films alluded to in the articles discussed up to this point might just as well have been novels. It is therefore worth looking in some detail at what has struck me as the most sustained attempt by a legal scholar to bring concepts and processes from the world of film directly to bear on the understanding of law and legal process without positioning those concepts as an accidentally celluloid version of literature. The work in question is that of Philip N. Meyer, two of whose essays in this area I will examine here.

Meyer's unusual strategy is to embrace "cinematic" as a master term: the cinematic, for Meyer, is robust and primary enough that it can serve as a point of reference or emulation for other regimes of narrative. Meyer's 1992 article "Law Students Go to the Movies" offers an account of and extensive reflections on a course (taught under law-and-literature auspices) in which he alternated novels and films as assigned texts.[44] By his own account, his reasons for proceeding in this manner were in part pragmatic: "requiring students to read a book a week is too heavy a load. A busy law student, however, exhausted from reading an overload of appellate cases, easily can view two movies in preparation for a seminar class."[45] But the turn to cinema also reflected a particular perspective on narrative film and its relation to trial law:

I chose movies as texts because of the similarity between trial and movie storytelling. Many popular storytellers, particularly filmmakers, have much to teach law students and valuable teaching themes are imbedded in popular movies. The aesthetic narrative constraints controlling the movie maker are akin to those controlling the trial attorney. Like the movie maker, the trial attorney is an oral cultural storyteller who tells fact-based narratives that convey a story and a particular vision of the world.[46]

Here, Meyer points up the specificity of cinema as a narrative and representational regime and assigns it a status comparable to that of literary production—not identical, but not subordinate. Indeed, he explicitly makes the comparison in the course of mapping out his cinematic focus: "The trial attorney, like the movie director and *unlike* the novelist, describes action in a shared external world. . . . Unlike a reader, the audience at trial or at the cinema is unable to turn back the pages and revisit the past. The story is told at one speed and, to effectively communicate, must be shaped to conform to shared narrative expectations of the entire audience."[47]

The suggestion that filmmakers and their audiences stand equidistant, in some sense, from a shared external world leaves room for questioning from the perspective of film theory (the matter of authorial presence being one of the most vexed). But whatever its theoretical ramifications, there is no doubt that Meyer's position moves film, in its complexity as a cognitive and cultural practice, to the center of his project: "Finally, cinema is the predominant mode of narrative storytelling in contemporary culture. Law students, attorneys and law professors are a product of this culture. . . . Additionally, . . . when operating in the narrative mode of thought, in contrast to the paradigmatic or analytical mode of thought, we perceive—literally see—causality in relationships that properly may be characterized as 'cinematic.'"[48]

This use of "cinematic" as a master term—rather than "literary," "textual," or "narrative"—is quite unusual in legal scholarship on film. Meyer himself follows up on it in his 1994 article "'Desperate for Love': Cinematic Influences upon a Defendant's Closing Argument to a Jury."[49] Here, he discusses a 1991 mob trial that he attended, analyzing in particular the defense attorney's closing argument for its "cinematic" influences and qualities: "The argument presented a three-part narrative structure akin to the three act classical dramatic structure as reconfigured in commercial film. The similarities are remarkable; it is as if the aesthetic concerns of popular cinematic storytelling had been adopted in shaping the trial and the closing argument that encapsulated the defendant's version of reality."[50]

This unmediated engagement on Meyer's part with the notion of the cinematic provides him with a somewhat whimsical idiom for his own synopsizing of the defense lawyer's closing argument ("Donovan cut to the next scene . . .")[51] and a very suggestive framework for serious reflection on the nature of courtroom argumentation and its position in the family tree of narrative practices. In particular, he introduces material from instructional texts on screenwriting, by way of suggesting that in certain key respects (character portrayal, thematic development) trial attorneys take their cue, in the first instance, not from literary convention but from film, where "characters seldom display the depth of literary characters"[52] and narrative developments are constrained by the priority of a small number of organizing themes. Moreover—and perhaps helpfully, when it comes to the inevitable matter of the disputability of any broad claim about the shallowness of characters in films—Meyer refers his argument back to the craft of screenwriting: the chief analogy is between the screenwriter and the attorney. This disposition of things takes some of the weight off the area of audience cognition and response. We may consider the characters in films we have seen to be complex, and yet Meyer's main point is that instructional texts on the craft of screenwriting say things like, "Their character traits have to be compressed and condensed. All non-essential character traits must be eliminated and then compacted—layered—into a denser form."[53]

In short, Meyer brings to the surface the historical fact of cinema—that is, the fact that much of what it means to say that we live in a narrative culture is that we live in a cinematic culture—and takes the notion of the cinematic seriously as a unit of meaning and a point of reference in the examination of other narrative practices. This is not to put his claims beyond dispute nor to suggest that no purpose can be served by other types of appropriation of film by law. But in its granting of gravity to the cinematic—in its treatment of law as cinema, rather than films as legal texts—Meyer's work differs decisively from the majority of such appropriations.

By the same token, Meyer's essays are somewhat anomalous. In what follows, I return to the mainstream—that is, I address the general thrust of the use of film by legal scholars from the perspective of film studies. The very rarity of an approach like Meyer's, which traffics in the cultural and narrative specificity of cinema, suggests the need for a close look at the majority practices of legal scholars who write about film.

Film < Law < Literature

In general, there is a close resemblance between law-and-film essays and law-and-literature essays. Without getting too biological or deterministic, I would claim at least some family connection. Most legal scholarship of the type we have looked at has, as its aim, the use of film (as exemplar, referent, teaching tool) to elucidate and enrich areas of legal practice and interpretation. In this sense, it is akin to, if not on every occasion a direct offshoot of, the law-and-literature movement.

There are also cases where the genealogy is made explicit; this is true, in particular, of a symposium published in the *Legal Studies Forum* in 1991 and dedicated to the topic of "Legal Reelism: Hollywood Films as Legal Texts."[54] Guest editor John Denvir opens the symposium with these remarks: "Ten years ago a special issue on 'Law And Literature' would have had to argue the jurisprudential merits of the project. Now that battle seems clearly won and we hear David Papke call for a fuller 'intertextuality,' an exploration of the intertwining of a wide variety of written and social texts relevant to the study of law. This collection of essays argues that the 'commercial' Hollywood film has a distinctive contribution to make to that enterprise."[55]

Denvir also contributed an essay to the symposium, namely, "Frank Capra's First Amendment," in which he argues that "Frank Capra's 1939 film comedy, *Mr. Smith Goes to Washington*, challenges [Justice] Holmes' conception of free speech, thereby deepening our understanding of the ideal of free speech and how it operates, or fails to operate, in American political culture."[56] Denvir delves into the underlying question of the use of an artifact of mass entertainment as a resource in legal scholarship (in effect, as a rhetorical weapon against Holmes) and, coming down in favor of such usage, mines the plot of *Mr. Smith* for behaviors, attitudes, and positions that may be brought to bear in the service of analyzing and criticizing the position of a Supreme Court justice on the matter of First Amendment rights.

In one sense, of course, it is gratifying to see attention being paid to film, as it had been to literature, by legal scholarship. However, a curious and somewhat disturbing asymmetry lurks in this apparent embrace. What we are invited to survey is a treatment of films *as legal texts*—and not, in any sense, legal texts, or law, *as film*. In other words, where law subordinates itself to *literature* (law and/in/*as* literature), film finds itself subordinated to law (film *as* legal text). This asymmetry may be expressed with the help of the mathematical "is less than" notation: film < law < literature. In other words, law and literature are things "as" which other things sometimes function. Film, however, while it can function "as" something else, cannot be functioned "as."

While it would not be appropriate to read this subordination of film into every essay on film by a legal scholar, it is not only in the *Legal Studies Forum* symposium that it surfaces or is implied. Even Meyer, whose engagement with cinematic issues is very deep, explains that his course "Law and Popular Storytelling" "probably was the only *Law and Literature* course to use movies as the primary texts and required course materials"; and he adds in a footnote: "None of the thirty-eight 'Law and Literature' courses surveyed [in a 1989 article by Elizabeth V. Gemmette] used films as primary texts in the curriculum."[57] One wants to ask, at the possible cost of sounding naïve, *Why would they?* Wouldn't that be, rather, the job of a law and *film* class? Is it so self-evident that any consideration of film by law students must take place under the auspices of—indeed, could not happen without—the law-and-literature movement?

Furthermore, film theory is not tapped by legal scholarship in anything like the way literary theory is. While the uses of fictional texts may be quite similar as between novels and films, we very rarely see law learning at the feet of Metz, Bazin, or Bordwell. There are, to be sure, occasional mentions of such writers, but clearly the primary flow of theoretical ideas is from literary theory to law and thence—perhaps—to film.

In the balance, at least for a film scholar, is the very solidity of the film studies discipline and its membership as an equal in the company of the disciplines with which it interacts and that choose to interact with it. A full evaluation of this state of affairs requires something more than a defensive reaction from film studies. But a defensive reaction—that is, a direct response to the relatively low ranking of film among neighboring disciplines—is not a bad place to start.

A Few Lines of Defense

While the imbalance in the "as" relationships works chiefly to the disadvantage of film, not even law stands above scrutiny in the matter of disciplinary fullness. As we saw earlier, C. R. B. Dunlop questions whether there really is an autonomous field of "law" legitimately separable from other scholarly enterprises. He issues some important warnings about the chief danger of interdisciplinary work—namely, the danger that it might not be done very well:

> Law students may rebel at the prospect of pharmacy professors attempting to teach the law of trusts; they may be equally concerned about law professors trying to explain literature, philosophy, or sociology. . . .
>
> . . . The pressure to do well is greater when one's readers or auditors know something of the discipline the scholar is expounding. The pressure is weaker when the law professor purports to discuss literature in a law classroom or in a legal periodical.[58]

A legal scholar who wants to write about literature, legal history, or legal philosophy must master literature, history, or philosophy. "Literature is literature," writes Dunlop, "whether taught in an English department or in a law school, and it raises all the questions of knowledge, methodology, and experience present for the teacher in an English department."[59] He emphasizes the need for erudition and connoisseurship as a minimal backdrop for participation by an outsider in a field such as literature. A law professor who wishes to write or lecture on *Bleak House*, for example, "will need to read as much of Dickens as possible, as well as works by his contemporaries and other writers. . . . Some knowledge of Victorian history . . . will be essential. . . . She will have to make at least a preliminary investigation of the enormous critical literature around *Bleak House* and Dickens' fiction as a whole."[60]

Legal scholars who write about film span a wide range of erudition and depth of research on the subject. The median, however, is fairly low. Part of this may have to do with the widespread notion that "everyone's an expert" when it comes to film. This is not to attribute to the authors of these particular articles any particular opinion on the academic legitimacy of film studies but only to suggest that film studies operates on a kind of honor system: since we all do, in fact, watch movies, and since most of us know a lot of films and talk a lot about film in many social contexts, the idea that talk about film should be left to experts has to be taken on faith. (The halfway figure of the journalistic film critic probably doesn't help here.)

One area where this body of work, as a whole, falls short of the best of film studies is in its heavy reliance on plot summaries and synopses. This is a tricky area. Certainly, synopsizing a plot is not a crime;

nor is it the case, of course, that film scholars never do it. Nor, moreover, is synopsizing a film in order to discuss it all that different from synopsizing an essay about film in order to discuss it. Nonetheless, it is rather telling that, while conducting inquiries into the very nature of narrative and representation, many of these essays uncritically assume that a verbal summary of a film can successfully stand in for the film—though many of the authors would vigorously question, at a theoretical and philosophical level, the same kind of substitution of word for event in the language of the courtroom. On the whole, plot description reigns, and there is relatively little attention to those aspects of the material and the experience of film that are *not* available by the mechanism of verbal paraphrase of the plot.

Moreover—again while concerned with the relativity of interpretation and meaning—many legal writers on film construct an extremely ideal spectator; that is, a spectator whose interpretations and reactions to a film can readily be predicted. Except in very probing essays like Sokolow's, we do not hear any echoes of developments in the area of reception studies in film—an area that has for a number of years been very central to film studies, certainly central enough that scholars operating according to Dunlop's criteria of interdisciplinary responsibility might be attuned to it.

An initial, defensive response, then, is certainly possible: as film scholars, we can find enough of mediocrity and out-of-touchness in these essays to enable us shrug off the film < law < literature slight. But as I indicated earlier, that is not the whole story. There are at least two further major concerns, and considerably more food for thought, for film scholars here.

To start with, film studies has privileged literature *over itself* as much as legal scholarship has privileged literature over film. Literature and literary theory consistently exert a tremendous pull. When other disciplines step back and generalize about themselves, we often see rapid recourse to notions of narrative, storytelling, mythmaking, and/or other basically literary forms (or forms that, at least, are perceived as basically literary). This is not, however, an easily charted us/them dichotomy; while "literary" and "verbal" are not synonyms, they are linked closely enough that no theorist making a case for the verbal basis of all narrative can fully afford to scoff at the granting of special status to literature. Still, to an extent alarming even to such a theorist, literary practice and theory definitely get the nod from film studies as well as from legal scholarship in the matter of artistic, cultural, and philosophical primacy.

Law, Film, and Teleology

There is also a second consideration that might give film scholars pause before we become too indignant about the Cinderella status assigned us by legal scholarship. While the essays I have examined here vary widely along the axis of the quality of film scholarship (and that of "attitude," perhaps), they all uniformly share another, very constant coefficient: the *use* of film in the service of a *legal* goal. There is an irreducible real-world component to law and legal education. This is not to say that there is consensus among scholars, practitioners, or students but rather that the process of education stands in a direct and, all things considered, extremely robust relation to subsequent professional work. Whatever they may think, say, and believe, these people know that they are going to operate within the legal system, and that is what their education is for—whether it consists of learning how to interpret authoritative texts according to old and unchanging principles or how to read imaginative literature for the sake of understanding the experiential and emotional aspects of the law. Moreover, law-and-literature advocates—those who would introduce novels and short stories into the syllabus—*share* this goal with their critics. The issue for the law-and-literature movement is not whether or not to provide students with a legal education but how to do it. It is of the greatest importance, in this connection, that legal scholarship, even as it borrows from or turns to literature, has the very constant and identifiable goal of education toward, or commentary upon, an existing professional regime. In other words, the law-and-literature approach represents a modification, but not an overturning, of an established order within which legal education is directly related to legal professionalism.

Legal studies, in other words, has a constant and identifiable telos. This is reflected in the explicitly school-related essays, such as Laurence's and Sokolow's, that either use film rhetorically or recount its use in the classroom as a tool for gaining access to important legal issues. It is also reflected in what might be called the more classically film-scholarly legal article, such as Sheffield's, that is not vastly different in form and agenda from film history written by film historians but that nonetheless makes connections with extrafilmic history of vital importance to the article and its audience. Indeed, the audience becomes the key here: as I suggested earlier, it may be in some cases that the publication venue and the targeted audience, as much as any other factor, determine the classification of the work as film scholarship or legal scholarship. Obviously, scholars from one field can research and read publications in another; but the weight of distribution and exposure of a law journal article will be toward academic lawyers, and that counts for something in the determination of the essay's identity. (I would add, however, that we need only rarely resort to this criterion. Most legal writing on film is quite distinct from most film scholarship.)

Vulgar as it may sound, one litmus test of the ways in which legal scholarship uses film for nonfilmic ends is the question, Would it matter if the author had entirely made up the films? We find a range of answers, which to some extent shadows the range of answers to, "Is this good film scholarship?" though not necessarily in every case.

It seems to me that Soifer could literally have made up *Casablanca.* This does not mean that his scholarship is weightless—in fact, on the contrary, it means that he has an important agenda that is not actually contingent on anything historical or real about *Casablanca* but that nonetheless makes use of it. Denvir could have invented *It's a Wonderful Life,* because in his article there is no actual engagement with anything about the film, other than a verbal synopsis of its plot. Interestingly, Sokolow actually does rewrite *Rashomon,* in a manner of speaking. He alludes to the film's "nineteenth-century setting" and almost writes the husband's death out of the script through his summary of the story as involving "a rape and murder told from four different points of view—those of the rapist, *the* victim, *the victim's* husband, and a passing woodcutter."[61]

The point here, however, is not to hunt for errors or superficiality on the part of legal scholars writing about film but rather to suggest that in many cases, from the point of view of the substantive *purpose* of the scholarship, *it would not matter* if the films had been invented or misrepresented. This, in my opinion, raises some very provocative questions for film studies. Meyer reports that a class sat around discussing the narrative structure of *Chinatown.* I, as a film scholar, would be unable to publish, in a film journal, a statement that my students sat around discussing the narrative structure of *Chinatown.* We assume our students do such things. Meyer reports it—and can report it—because it is a stepping-stone on the way to something else, namely, some timely and probing remarks about *legal* pedagogy.

The question for film scholars then becomes: if legal scholars can do what we do, but do it with a further purpose (a purpose that, moreover, retains its purposefulness, whether or not these legal scholars are good film scholars), should we wonder whether what we are doing is incomplete? Is film studies, performed for its own sake, lacking an entire dimension of purpose?

Law borrows from literature and film in the service of reaching its own telos. Film studies borrows, too, but its borrowings virtually amount to its substance. Unlike legal education, film studies has no clear-cut relation with an overriding and constant goal. The study of film is, or hopes it is, a valuable academic discipline in its own right. To be sure, there is a real-world professional practice with which it has a relation, though a less self-explanatory and more troubled relation than that which legal education enjoys with legal practice: namely, of course, filmmaking. But as anyone who has earned a Ph.D. in film *studies* knows, there is an endless process of convincing the world (generally at the proverbial or not-so-proverbial cocktail party) that what one is doing is not a sorry substitute for filmmaking but is, rather, an intellectual and professional pursuit with its own substance, its own professional organizations, its own publications, and its own history. Filmmaking is not something I know very much about firsthand, nor is it something on which I expect to exert much influence. The main role it plays in my intellectual life is to serve as an impressive, substantive pursuit, the belated realization of my noninvolvement with which causes embarrassment to people who feel they have uncovered a guilty secret.

Indeed, many of us do teach history and theory to future filmmakers. In teaching courses on film and broadcast history to very "techie" students, I find myself trying to sell the courses by making a case for their importance even to people who are going into production rather than academia. Still, I invariably feel that I am clamping the two areas together through willpower and necessity; I do not *really* know that camera operators who have never seen *The American Friend* are any less qualified or competent than those who have. But if film scholars do not breed filmmakers in quite the way that legal scholars breed lawyers, one might regain the analogy by suggesting that film theorists train other film theorists—and, after all, if film studies is a legitimate pursuit, then so is the pursuit of educating people in it.

We have, then, in both law and film the pairing of *profession* and *educational process*—indeed, in film we seem to have two such pair-ings, namely, one each in the two cases of film production and film studies. But the profession/education pairing in the legal area operates under the governance of a telos that, certainly in the large, the world of film education/profession does not. If there are counterarguments to be made—that is, if we were to claim teleology of a socially and politically charged kind for film-related career cycles—we would certainly develop such counterarguments in connection with film*making*, not film *stud-ies.* After all, a filmmaker actually does have a shot at influencing thought and raising consciousness. Film studies, for all the political and ideological excitement it displays at the atomic level, seems to me to share with almost all of its sibling academic disciplines the inability to have much to do with politics and social awareness on any larger scale. It is not for lack of desire or trying; rather, it is a matter of what the institution actually *is,* as opposed to what, in some parallel universe, its members might have done with their political acuity.

This may be why debate in film studies about paradigms and meth-odology so often feels sterile and circular—sometimes most so when it is most ardent and revisionist. Whatever type of film studies we engage in, we are not keeping innocent people out of jail or helping to revise laws; nor will the earth fly off its axis if someone performs a close tex-tual analysis of a film during a time when such analysis has been de-clared "dead" by the exponents of some other, supposedly incompat-ible approach. By the same token, we are also not sending people to the electric chair. Lawyers are not nobler than film theorists, but their stud-ies have a goal outside of themselves, a goal with, at least potentially, a real-life version of the political engagement and power that scholars in fields like film try to attach to their fields, whether it sticks or not.

Inasmuch as film studies does not have a readily identifiable telos, film professors, in my experience, do not use films to instill understand-ing or values that will be used for some other purpose. We generally do not say to students, "Let's talk about this film because it contains themes that will play into activities X, Y, and Z in which you will en-gage as a result of this education." It would be very hard to imagine the equivalent, in film studies, of Camilleri's use of the short story to sug-gest aspects of the law—that is, the use of literature to explore some-thing other than literature and specifically something vocational (rather than generally humanistic). What would we even "use" in this way: films? short stories? theoretical texts? And what regime would we be illuminating: film studies itself? filmmaking? spectatorship? I can imagine, just, using a theoretical text to suggest that theory can be more humanistic or more compassionate; but still, what I am doing is training film theorists, and it is a closed system.

Ironically, it is easier for legal scholars to use films for pedagogical purposes than it is for film scholars—at least the former have more of a purpose, with relation to their professional activities, in doing so. In law, there is something at stake: it really matters whether future lawyers, judges, and legislators have been called upon (via film or otherwise) to reflect on certain matters. This does not mean that there is no value in politicized film studies; since one functions as a political person, and a person within the legal system, an emphasis by film studies on political issues has an effect. But the inner economy of learning and practice is very different from that of legal pedagogy and training. In short, by studying film *without* putting it in the kind of context it finds in legal studies, we either demonstrate that studying film is a legitimate academic goal in itself or we fail, precisely, to do so.

Closing Argument

Dunlop points out that law schools are branching out more and more into other things and that there are growing pains—a lot of resistance to this expansion. This is really an ontological debate: if law actually *is* literature (rather than just masquerading *as* literature, or whatever), then presumably it should be treated that way. In the case of film scholarship, what pains we feel are still birth pains. Film studies is a bastard discipline, and some of its interdisciplinariness, perhaps, is a consequence of the fact that, historically, it has had to struggle for an identity. Film courses have been taught in departments of, inter alia, English, art history, American studies, comparative literature, German, and communication. Relatively few schools have departments or even full programs devoted to film. The point is that law and film seem to be going in opposite directions: law, trying to branch out; film, either trying to consolidate or, in what may turn out to be a dance of death, giving up on consolidation and embracing the status of bastardy. Film scholars are expected to read pretty much everything except film scholarship, and in fact the dialogue we maintain with other disciplines is tremendously self-effacing. We confess contingency, whereas legal scholars test their wings. "Film < X," we seem only too ready to proclaim, "for any X."

Inasmuch as this book is about connections and bridges between law and film, it is worth noting that finding those connections can mean different things to different disciplines. Moreover, a lot may depend on who finds the connections. Law professors find connections between films and legal theory and/or pedagogy. A film scholar looks for connections between those law professors' acts of finding and the finding of theoretical and/or pedagogical value in films by *film* scholars—and finds things rather different. To be sure, there may be some (cold) comfort available in the fact that legal scholarship on film does not add up to a cogent contribution to anything we might call film studies, whether we define that discipline by content, scope, positioning, methodology, or even audience. Yet there is at least as much (cold) food for thought in the contemplation of matters of teleology and purpose as from one entire sphere of practice to another.

Notes

1. C. R. B. Dunlop, "Literature Studies in Law Schools," *Cardozo Studies in Law and Literature* 3.1 (Spring–Summer 1991): 65–66.

2. Ibid., 67.

3. Ibid.

4. Ibid., 69.

5. Ibid., 63.

6. Ibid., 75.

7. Marijane Camilleri, "Lessons in Law from Literature: A Look at the Movement and a Peer at Her Jury," *Catholic University Law Review* 39.2 (Winter 1990): 557–94.

8. Ibid., 574.

9. Ibid., 559–60.

10. Ibid., 564.

11. Ibid., 565–66.

12. Ibid., 567–68.

13. Ibid., 581.

14. Ibid., 584.

15. Ibid., 589.

16. Aviam Soifer, "Complacency and Constitutional Law," *Ohio State Law Journal* 42.1 (1981): 383.

17. Ric Sheffield, "Taking Exception to Six Decades on Film: A Social History of Women Lawyers in Popular Culture, 1930 to 1990," *Loyola of Los Angeles Entertainment Law Journal* 14.1 (1993): 73–114.

18. Ibid., 108.

19. Ibid., 78–79.

20. Ibid., 80–81.

21. Ibid., 84–85.

22. Ibid., 87–89.

23. Ibid., 111.

24. Soifer, 386–87.

25. Ibid., 394.

26. Ibid., 402.

27. Ibid., 405.

28. Ibid., 383.

29. Robert Laurence, "Last Night While You Prepared for Class I Went to See *Light of Day:* A Film Review and a Message to My First-Year Property Students, Annotated for My Colleagues," *Journal of Legal Education* 39.1 (March 1989): 87–96.

30. Ibid., 87n1.

31. Ibid., 88.

32. Ibid., 88–89.

33. Ibid., 89–90.

34. Ibid., 91n8, 94n17.

35. David Simon Sokolow, "From Kurosawa to (Duncan) Kennedy: The Lessons of *Rashomon* for Current Legal Education," *Wisconsin Law Review* 1991.5 (September–October 1991): 969–86.

36. Ibid., 969.

37. Ibid., 971.

38. Ibid., 969.

39. Ibid., 974–75.

40. Ibid., 977.

41. Ibid., 978.

42. Ibid., 980.

43. One might drum up quite a little theory about films that spark isomorphic reactions in their viewers. *Rashomon* seems to make people argue about narrative versions. *Vertigo* (at least for some of us) leads to long ramblings around San Francisco in search of historically charged locations.

44. Philip N. Meyer, "Law Students Go to the Movies," *Connecticut Law Review* 24.3 (Spring 1992): 893–913.

45. Ibid., 898.

46. Ibid., 896–97.

47. Ibid., 897–98.

48. Ibid., 898.

49. Philip N. Meyer, "'Desperate for Love': Cinematic Influences upon a Defendant's Closing Argument to a Jury," *Vermont Law Review* 18.3 (Spring 1994): 721–49.

50. Ibid., 722–23.

51. Ibid., 735.

52. Ibid., 740.

53. Ibid., 740n60.

54. *Legal Reelism: The Hollywood Film as Legal Text*, ed. John Denvir, special issue of *Legal Studies Forum* 15.3 (1991) served as the basis for *Legal Reelism: Movies as Legal Texts*, ed. John Denvir (Urbana: University of Illinois Press, 1996).

55. John Denvir, "From the Guest Editor," *Legal Studies Forum* 15.3 (1991): 195.

56. John Denvir, "Frank Capra's First Amendment," *Legal Studies Forum* 15.3 (1991): 255, 263.

57. Meyer, 894, 894n5 (emphasis added).

58. Dunlop, 81.

59. Ibid.

60. Ibid., 81–82. There is an interesting twist here: in a sense, Dunlop is arguing more from (and for) the sanctity of literary theory than legal pedagogy; that is, he is protecting it as some kind of identifiable and integral entity while arguing for the loosening of the borders of *legal* pedagogy.

61. Sokolow, 975n39, 975 (emphasis added).

7

The Forensics of Film Reception

A Likely Story!

A treatment of the centrality of probabilistic reasoning and judgment to the regimes of film and law might conceivably belong in the part of this book devoted to parallels between the two regimes, rather than here among the regimes of writing. Except that it is not just a matter of "legal narrative revolves around probabilism and plausibility, and so does filmic narrative." There turns out to be something going on beyond, or other than, a parallel stake in plausibility. That something, moreover, turns out to have more to do with film than with law, and more to do with response to film than with film production or content.

What might have been a brick in the wall of the "two-regimes-in-parallel" survey involves instead primarily a close examination of certain tendencies and practices—rhetorical, responsive, both written and oral but at least largely written—observable in the orbit of film. As I will explain, these observations have a place here, despite the fact that they concern film more than they concern law, because one of the key traits of what is being observed is film's rhetorical, legalistic, and *forensic* qualities.

The centrality of plausibilistic reasoning and judgment to law, in my view, is a done deal, so I will elaborate only briefly on it. My focus here will be film. The role of plausibility in the regime of commercial film requires detailed consideration, partly because it is not as obvious as its counterpart in law and partly because, as I will argue, it turns out to be extremely important.

Legal procedure depends on the exercise of judgment on narratives, largely taking the form of the evaluation of stories on the criterion of plausibility. It is familiar enough that courtroom witnesses produce conflicting testimony; that judges and juries must reconcile or choose among conflicting versions; that plausibility governs much of that reconciling activity; and that lawyers strive, among other things, to demonstrate implausibility in testimony. Bennett and Feldman perform the salutary act of positioning the strife over plausibility largely in the symbolic world of the story:

> Judgments based on story construction are, in many important respects, unverifiable in terms of the reality of the situation that the story represents. Adjudicators judge the plausibility of a story according to certain structural relations among symbols in the story. Although documentary evidence may exist to support most symbolizations in a story, both the teller and the interpreter of a story *always* have some margin of control over the definition of certain key symbols. Therefore, stories are judged in terms of a combination of the documentary or "empirical" warrants for symbols and the internal structural relations among the collection of symbols presented in the story. In other words, we judge stories according to a dual standard of "did it happen that way?" and "could it have happened that way?"[1]

Plausibility thus adheres to the stories of the legal regime (or not) as a function of their internal relations and properties as well as by the criterion of agreement with prior or external data, which can include the hearers' social prejudices and ethical predispositions as well as admitted evidence.

The regime of plausibility in law, by this light, centers not on the material of legal narratives but on their reception and evaluation. Stories themselves are not plausible or implausible: they are candidates for inclusion in one of two critical categories, the appropriate category to be determined by structural and semantic exegesis. It is by dint of a rhetoric of *response* that narratives gain membership in one of these categories or the other.

Making the case for our film culture's obsession with plausibility involves something different but disarmingly simple—namely, pointing out the fact that commentary on film (whether published or spoken from friend to friend) frequently tends to dwell on matters of plausibility. Since I am putting the spotlight on what might otherwise be taken as the least significant, throwaway banter imaginable, I wish to be entirely clear about it: I mean, quite literally, the kinds of conversation that take place on the way out of the movie theater or in response to a friend asking about a movie.

In exploring this phenomenon, I shall draw heavily from journalistic film reviews, but what is said here about the significance of this type of commentary has application to many manifestations of it in many forms. Hence its designation as a "regime of writing" should be understood as standing in for an even wider sweep.

> How did an Aurora and a Rudyard come to christen their only child Emma? . . . Aurora Greenway does not seem to have read a book in all the 30 years of the screen narrative. Yet she has a Renoir in her bedroom. . . . Well, I have been standing at New York checkout counters for about half a century, but I have never in all my life heard anyone yell out from the end of the line to the front of the line that he had turned down someone's second mortgage. [Andrew Sarris on *Terms of Endearment*][2]

> What Yentl studies with such devotion is the set of rules that keep her in her place as surely as leg irons and padlocks. If she is in search of the "freedom" that learning will give her, why doesn't she just look for it when her father dies? [Sheila Benson on *Yentl*][3]

> Why the damned box [i.e., the Ark of the Covenant] could not have been opened in Egypt is one more mystery. [Robert Asahina on *Raiders of the Lost Ark*][4]

> Garrison and his wife (Sissy Spacek) are seen in bed dismissively shaking their heads over a television documentary which attacked Garrison's procedures. In fact, these charges were taken much more seriously than *JFK* indicates. [Philip Strick on *JFK*][5]

> They talk in a post–Valley Speak mode ("dude," "cowabunga"), even though they are ostensibly New Yorkers. [Jami Bernard on *Teenage Mutant Ninja Turtles*][6]

> Hard to take your eyes off her, even to glance at fine appearances by Kurt Russell as her boyfriend and Cher as her house-sharing chum, a lesbian. But the real Karen had no such lesbian chum, and so on and so forth. Better outright fiction than this reasonless hybrid, where the sense of wasted talent is devastating. [John Coleman on *Silkwood*][7]

What these remarks have in common is that they find factually *against the cinema* on a variety of probabilistic, empirical, and/or historical grounds. In this they illustrate a much wider film-cultural obsession with plausibility, an obsession materialized in the incessant questioning we read and hear as to whether or not something in a film "would have happened"; assertions that a character "would not have done that"; protests against lapses in continuity and psychological motivation; and more narrowly targeted complaints about a film's historical or biographical accuracy.

An analysis of the prominence of plausibility in reactions to film might begin and end without any comparison with law. Such an analysis would fit nicely into a theory of filmic pleasure because it is an index—and a very talkative one—of *dis*pleasure. But there is more at stake, and what we will encounter is nothing less than the matter of the power of narrative film. I have suggested that the analogue to legal power is filmic pleasure. It turns out, however, that film has power of its own—and that its power hinges on narrative and on plausibility.

All the critics' statements I have quoted use the same rhetorical strategy: they express the opinion, or the concern, that a film *got something wrong*, as measured against one or more yardsticks, readily to hand, of historical, behavioral, or social actuality. Moreover, and very importantly, these are *public* utterances. These points are true, too, of the larger body of spoken statements and observations cut from the same plausibilistic cloth. In short, we find, in the aggregate, an abundance of public (spoken, written) responses to a vast array of particulars of narrative films, those responses taking the form of apparent findings of *error*, as revealed to plausibilistic, probabilistic reasoning.

I shall refer to statements of this kind as "corrective," in the sense that they take issue with elements of theme and plot posited by the films they concern; and I shall refer to the practice overall—that is, the practice of making such corrective pronouncements, of publicly attacking a film for having erred in its representation of reality—as "forensic criticism." Corrective remarks, examined in situ as public, material utterances (rather than evaluated for their truth value, which is not the point), constitute a kind of cross-examination of film; position the critic (the corrector) as an investigator into underlying truths; and imply a lateral and adversarial relationship between filmic narrative and public response to it. Put another way, forensic criticism amounts to testimony *against* films—public acts of discrediting, reproach, and exposure.

The corrective response is neither a recent development (as suggested by a review of Griffith's *Lonely Villa* that objects: "In real life, burglars could have smashed through all the obstacles with which this trio were confronted in one-tenth the time"[8]) nor an exclusively journalistic practice. Indeed, this discussion of forensic criticism bears on a great deal of everyday, spontaneous, and informal discussion of film. Forensic criticism is probably *most* familiarly and prolifically a casual, friend-to-friend, oral practice. Examples drawn from journalistic criticism simply represent a point of entry to an issue that pertains to everyday discourse and to the most broad-based questions of subject-film relations.[9]

As a discursive practice, forensic criticism of film stands at the intersection of a number of diverse topics. One might examine similarly inflected criticism aimed at other narrative forms (plays, books, operas); or in connection with other, noncorrective kinds of response to film; or in the context of a general theory of media consumption (in which forensic criticism might figure only as a footnote); or as a chapter in the history of probabilistic argumentation above and beyond film. Moreover, forensic criticism, and whatever impulse drives it, is amazingly tenacious. I know of no one who is "above" it, in respect of film-theoretical attainment or seniority. Nor am I aware of any inverse correlation between the overall amount of such theorizing in the world and the vigor of the corrective impulse it embodies; that is, theory cannot banish it or wish it away.

Forensic criticism spans a great deal of subject matter. Virtually anything represented in a film may be targeted for this kind of attack—plots, sets, actions, behaviors. Forensic criticism is practiced continuously along a broad spectrum of content, easily and indifferently encompassing the trivial and the significant. In this respect, it is logically equivalent to other responsive or critical activities such as quoting, forgetting, or recommending—all of which, similarly, may be exercised on texts, or textual passages, regardless of subject matter or content. We do not determine whether or not an utterance constitutes a "recommendation" of a film by scrutinizing the subject matter of the film it refers to; similarly, subject matter does not play a role in the process of determining whether a given verbal statement is or is not a corrective remark.

Aspects of Forensic Criticism

Forensic Criticism as Argumentation   Forensic criticism is a type of verbal response to narrative film, and verbal response to narrative film largely takes the form of renarration—that is, summarizing, retelling, recounting, synopsizing. Films narrate, and we, the respondents to films, narrate again—in fact, we narrate across the same referential space as that traversed by the film. We do this every time we whisper the essentials of the plot to a friend who has arrived late to the theater. Up to a point, forensic criticism is another form of such renarration. But it is a renarration with a special relation to film. Most retelling, synopsizing, and summarizing *agrees with* (or is conventionally taken as agreeing with) the filmic narrative of which it is, so to speak, another version. We may safely assume that the whispered plot "agrees" with the film it summarizes. Forensic criticism, however, renarrates a film but *conflicts* with it. The corrective remark constitutes a new version, but it is a skeptical and therefore competing and hostile one.

Any focused consideration of forensic criticism as such takes us directly to the matter of the balance of narratorial and predicative power between film and its respondents. Corrective criticism is argumentative. It involves not only a lateral positioning of the respondent as a narrator with the right to narrate across the film's referential space—a common enough thing—but the conferral upon the respondent of the status of debater with the film in the matter of the very events the film has predicated. It is as if, the film having presented one opinion, the corrector takes the floor and presents another—all with respect to some external event, fact, or narrative referent and all addressed to a third, arbitrating party. The forensic remark's primary concern is not the communication of an opinion about the film as a finished, static object but the setting straight of a (supposedly) noncontingent factual record distorted by the film. (See, again, the examples, each of which proofs the film against external commonplaces and topicalities.)

Many instances of forensic criticism are unremarkable and banal, which is all the more reason why we should take the very fact of forensic criticism—the fact that a film's respondent may usurp the space of the narrative—as a caution against too easy an acceptance or oversimplification of the ways in which film wields predicative and normative power. Whatever the real nature of the influence of film on the social imaginary, the practice of forensic criticism suggests that it is something other than dictatorial. If film were purely predicative, and its consumers purely absorbent, then it is fair to guess that the contentious, corrective remarks that comprise forensic criticism would literally not form themselves in the human mind.

Forensic criticism consists of statements that fault films for differing from reality. Its very existence therefore implies, and rests on, the position that the relationship between reality and representation is quantifiable, open to verbal description, and *potentially reducible to zero.* In other words, if a film can be taken to task for getting things wrong, then there must be such a thing as a film that gets everything right. Moreover, forensic criticism *seems* to involve a surrender of narratorial power by the film to the respondent. In fact, it is really one clause ("You have the right to contest what I narrate") in the massive, scrappy, sometimes highly unstable pact between the commercial cinema and its respondents.

In this light, I submit that the role played by forensic criticism is, first and foremost, that of diversion—that is, something included in the pact for the purpose (or, if one prefers, with the effect) of drawing attention away from the exclusion of something else. The minor skirmishes and faultfinding represented by forensic criticism serve as decoys away from what might otherwise develop into a more penetrating demystification of film or unmasking of its constructive strategies. Of course, we do not lack for highly accomplished deconstructions of the narrative cinema; but the corrective response perpetually renews itself and persists as a reflex, even where it has been logically argued out of existence. Forensic criticism is not a weapon but a pacifier *disguised* as a weapon, and there may be a more than incidental relationship between the very existence of such criticism and the fact that film, historically, has enjoyed license to arbitrate the social imaginary. Narrative film (the commercial regime, here, taking its cue from the celluloid substance) has learned to bend before it breaks. Forensic criticism seems to dissent but in fact establishes an ideological partnership with film, always negotiated on the latter's terms: we're in this together, says the cinema, but I've got the camera.

Forensic Criticism as Rhetoric Forensic criticism is argumentative, public, material; an occasional discourse, often ardent and declamatory; something addressed to someone with the goal of persuasion. It is, in short, *rhetorical.* Its tone and technique convey the unmistakable impression—despite its opponent's being an inanimate and finished artifact—that its basic stance is that of a participant in a debate, appealing to the judgment, sense, and love of logic of its auditors.[10]

Inasmuch as my concern here is with the practices and texts of forensic criticism, not with the rightness or wrongness of any forensic response in particular, it makes sense to follow this rhetorical thread. To start with, many forensically critical utterances, including several of the examples already introduced, are issued in the form of rhetorical questions.

But there is no reason to stop there . . .

argumentum ex concessis: Reasoning that the conclusion of an argument is sound, on the basis of the truth of the premises of one's opponent.[11]

Throughout, hausfrau Duvall has been limned as so dull-spirited that she can scarcely follow the images dancing across her TV set, much less commune with the ectoplasm holed up in the guest rooms—so why does she start seeing these (possibly imaginary) phantoms herself? [Stephen Harvey on *The Shining*][12]

apodioxis: Rejecting an argument indignantly as impertinent or false.

How are we supposed to react when realistic-seeming beatings don't leave a mark on one man but turn another into bloody hamburger? [Sheila Benson on *Miller's Crossing*][13]

enantiosis or *contrarium:* One of two opposite statements is used to prove the other.

And something goes badly adrift with the switches from voice-over to singing to camera: why, in the name of likelihood, should Yentl—on a last boat out—warble mutely when solitary by the ship's rail, only to stride stridently through an apparently deaf throng of fellow-passengers? [John Coleman on *Yentl*][14]

reductio ad absurdum or *antistrephon:* An argument that turns one's opponent's arguments or proofs to one's own purposes.

Writer-director David Lynch's new film, *Blue Velvet,* is supposed to be set in typical small town America; it might as well have been set on Mars. Either Lynch is pulling our leg from the start or he doesn't have the slightest idea about how to portray a realistic small town. [Kenneth M. Chanko on *Blue Velvet*][15]

The association between such critical pronouncements and familiar rhetorical forms occasionally finds overt expression:

My problem with *For Keeps* is a big one. Everything's presented just as the [accidentally conceived] baby is: in a cute and lovable, endearing little package. The few problems are more or less easily overcome, the folks all come around, and after a bumpy start the future looks rosy and love conquers all. But love doesn't conquer all. Ask any of the kids involved in America's ten- to twenty-thousand unwanted teenage pregnancies a week. This film's a comic fairy-tale, but the reality of movie-making, like the reality of teenage sex, calls for a little responsibility. End of *sermon.*[16]

As with rhetoric generally, the goal of corrective remarks of this type is persuasion. But there is more going on than a critic trying to "persuade" readers to see, or not see, a given film. The persuasive agenda of forensic criticism encompasses social realities at large; the goal is to persuade the reader/auditor that certain things are the case about the world, and that the film has lied.[17]

Indeed, there is more to the relationship between correction and rhetoric than the former's argumentative tone or figurative richness. There is also a paradox. In an elegant two-page summary of the history of Western discourse, Tzevetan Todorov argues that "for twenty-five centuries men have tried to convince one another that reality is a sufficient reason of speech; for twenty-five centuries, men have had to keep reconquering the right to perceive language." Within the history of that struggle, rhetoric falls firmly on the side of the perceptible. "To win the trial," Todorov writes, describing the supposed birth of rhetoric in the ancient Sicilian judicial system, "it is more important to speak well than to have behaved well. . . . discourse, narrative, ceases to be, in the speaker's consciousness, a docile reflection of events and acquires an independent value. Thus words are not simply the transparent names of things, they form an autonomous entity governed by its own laws and susceptible of being judged for itself."[18] Rhetoric, he explains, arose in tandem with the ability to perceive language and has, as a study and a practice, weighed in against the tendency to understand language as transparent and reality as available through and indifferent to it.

Forensic criticism is rhetorical: a material, public, persuasive, and, in Todorov's sense, perceptible discourse. At the same time, however, its very existence argues for a belief in consummate representation, for the *possibility* of the essential presence of the referent-event in the narrative. Thus the paradox. Making allowances for the fact that the present discussion involves mixed media—that is, that film is not homogeneously verbal while forensic criticism is—we can take a cue from Todorov's summary and make the observation that the practice of forensic criticism presents the paradox of *a rhetoric*—an opaque, "perceptible" discourse—*whose argumentative efforts are tirelessly devoted to affirming the potential transparency of representation.*

The Ethics of Forensic Criticism

The forensic critic—the actual person who engages in the practice, whether it be you, me, or Andrew Sarris—functions as arbiter between two versions of a film. Both versions are mental rather than material. One is the mental residuum of the film itself—the memory, the film rendered logomorphic. The other is a kind of ideal—what the film would have been had it not lapsed in point of plausibility. The arbiter conducts an ongoing proof of one version against the other, a kind of holding of the two up to the light, to see if they match. Should this proof encounter a snag (e.g., should the residual version indicate people behaving one way at a checkout counter, the ideal version another), there arises the corrective impulse and, ultimately, a pronouncement, an utterance: something oblique to *both* versions—in fact, a new version.

We all travel from the position of film-time viewer—that is, arbiter—to the position of speaker about a film, at least sometimes. The passage from arbiter to *corrector* is a passage from compliant synoptist of the film to public, forensic adversary. It may be that the corrective reaction to a film (the experience of thinking that a film has gotten something wrong, or realizing that we think so) is involuntary. But corrective criticism itself is not, for it issues from a decision not to have narrated what the film narrated, and it manifests itself in a public *refusal* of the film. In this respect, forensic criticism is always *ethical*, always a drawing of the line, always a refusal *by someone* to narrate "this" except under protest.

There is often a more than faint element in forensic criticism of the demonstration, affirmation, even flaunting of the critic's superiority (to the film) as logician. I would argue, in fact, that in many cases it is not wrong to posit such a demonstration as the *principal* motivation for corrective criticism and the ostensible content of the corrective remark as incidental. Sarris on checkout counters might be a suitable example here; the gesture of rhetorical display, which evaluates to a self-distanciation of the respondent from the film, might be understood as the chief impetus for the correction, while the specific subject matter of the remark serves only as fodder. The imperative here is that of standing up to the film, claiming parity with it, arguing against it, retelling it—something very different from modestly, altruistically setting the record straight.

If forensic criticism is a refusal to (re)narrate compliantly, what exactly is compliant (re)narration, and what can we learn from it about its refusal? It is worth looking at this question in detail—even if part of the answer is: "It by definition entails the absence of critically corrective response, and the details don't matter."

Consider the following comments about Brian De Palma's *Blow Out:*

1. After wreaking havoc, Travolta gets into an ambulance.
2. "After the havoc Travolta has wreaked in that Liberty Day parade (a dreamlike and rather delicious scene of mayhem in which no one is really hurt), how is it that there is not *one* policeman in or near his ambulance?"[19]
3. After wreaking havoc in that Liberty Day parade, Travolta gets into an ambulance. There are no policeman around, because there has been a gang disturbance nearby and all the available officers have been called away.

I would like to consider examples 1 and 3 as transformations of Benson's corrective remark—specifically, if speculatively, to consider what would have been involved in such a transformation and how the (non)existence of examples 1 and 3 might throw the significance of the actual corrective remark into higher relief. Examples 1 and 3 demonstrate that compliant wording is always available: as a function of rhetoric (at the moment of expression), it is never *necessary* to correct. That is only part of the story, however. There is also, and chiefly, the fact that the forensically critical turning point is (I believe) something that happens *during* the process of viewing. The material remark is not something whose characteristics are entirely decided on at the moment of writing or utterance; rather, the remark has, or behaves as if it has, a robust connection to something perceived and decided during the screening.

Indeed, we might experimentally turn the tables and put the question, If it is cognitively possible to find a story *that is not contradicted by the film* and that, at the same time, absolves the film of what would otherwise be a correctable representation, why does such a story *not occur* to the spectator as one of the possible hypotheses (to borrow a phrase from Constructivist theory) tested for validity in the course of viewing? For instance, example 3 is a compliant synopsis; the film does not explicitly denote the nonoccurrence of a gang disturbance. Furthermore, it lets the film off the hook (i.e., obviates any corrective response) and, from the point of view of mental processes, presumably could have occurred to Benson, and she could have used it. Why, then, didn't she?

We may not be able to get at this question fully without a full-blown theory of textual determinism—that is, of what is and is not "in" a film. I am steering clear of elaborating such a theory here, partly because to do so at any length would be digressive and partly because I would like to suggest that we can say at least something about correction (and its ethical aspect in particular) without one. For the record, I am quite relativistic on the issue and would not be satisfied to resort to the explanation that the events spelled out in example 3 are not in the film (although as a viewer I believe them not to be). At the same time, it is not only pragmatic but theoretically sound to grant that for each respondent *something* is in the film, and we should probably be asking what a consideration of the three examples might tell us, in general, about correction and its alternatives as after-the-fact rhetoric. Let us take as our starting point and center of gravity—the seesaw parallel to the ground—Benson's remark, together with the cognitive, precorrective response we can assume to have prefigured it. Let us posit further that Benson *could have* come out with any of the three remarks. I suggest that the three show us important options available in the aftermath of a corrective reaction to a film. Example 2 is, of course, classic forensic criticism: rhetorical, declamatory, argumentative. Example 1 represents a kind of retreat from the consummation of correction, a stripping away of the rhetorical barbs that do not allow the narrative to flow freely (i.e., that detain it and punish it for its mendacity). Example 3 is a kind of conspiratorial darning of the text, a replenishment of narrative information where there was none—or, to be textually nondeterministic, where the respondent did not perceive any. (And I do predicate that Benson did not perceive the story this way.) The options, in sum, are these: to correct the film; to retreat from conflict with the film; or to *cover* for the film.

Retreat is ethically below par in relation to the full-force corrective impulse. Of course, in terms of actual retellings, it may have its place; Benson may not have performed the same forensic act in summarizing the movie to friends (if she did so), and we can imagine situations in which a corrective impulse would need to be stifled (for instance, two-line plot summaries for television movie listings—which, to be sure, are for the most part responses to other movie listings rather than to screenings of films).

Covering for the film (as in example 3) is another matter. Having brought the rhetorical possibility of covering to the surface, I would suggest that the ethics of correction may be understood in large part as a *refusal* to do this—that is, the refusal to make life easy for the film, as well as the refusal to break with one's own intuitive response for the sake of making the film look good. We might even speak of the refusal of our film culture to have thought of doing this. In that light, it is certainly an artificial way to look at the process; however, it is instructive to consider that there could be a cultural imperative—an ethical imperative—to protect films, and perhaps there are even cases where publicists and other apologists have performed precisely such rhetorical acts of covering, even where their corrective faculties have told them better. (Many of us can dimly remember arguments with friends where one party, more smitten by a film than the other, might have come up with some fairly non-self-evident plot elements in the interest of refuting correction.)

A couple of key points arise from this exercise. First, the ethics of correction involve refusal of complicity—not so much at the cognitive stage, where that refusal is automatic, but at the later stage of rhetorical action—and a concomitant, affirmative *decision* to perform the public act of correction. Second, this example demonstrates the desirability of examining and evaluating forensic criticism as much in situ as possible, because it (and commentary about it) only makes sense when it takes into account the relations among the forensic critic, the act of viewing, and the response—that is, the materiality of all three, as well as their fusion. That is why an abstract argument about what is in the film misses the point. A discussion of forensic criticism needs to be able to slide along a nonfixed scale of textual determinism. Sheila Benson might have been someone who thought there was a gang disturbance in *Blow Out*. She might, nonetheless, have corrected the film on the grounds that gangs do not normally act up at parades. Examples 1, 2, and 3 would have looked a lot different—but they would have related to each other similarly and made the same point about the positioning, actions, and refusals of the corrector.

I would add that this need for flexibility also accounts for why we can almost, but not quite, define forensic criticism as a side effect of the selection of preferred or likely readings. Such a description would consider correction as a refusal, as a service to the film, to do the work necessary to create a version (such as example 3) that is clearly not any kind of likely reading (clearly eccentric with respect to the semantic target of the text). This is, to be sure, a tempting alternative to textual determinism. But the matter of likely readings—as well as the ethical significance of the forensically critical response—is quite fluid. It may be that forensic readings are best understood as unlikely or minority responses, at least in some cases: anyone who has watched a movie about the law with a lawyer, or a movie about an orchestra with a musician, or a movie about a university with an academic, . . . knows that correction is relative to the corrector. The lawyer watching the law film and complaining because it did not get courtroom procedure right might indeed see the noncorrective response as eccentric—and might shun it as a retreat from an ethical imperative.

The Politics of Forensic Criticism   If we grant that the very possibility of forensic criticism implies an unsuspectedly greater power of film to arbitrate the social imaginary, must we then conclude that there is no point protesting against offensive, misleading, or degrading representations and images or that to do so is, in terms of the balance of power, counterproductive? To put it confessionally: have I, through logic and/ or sophistry, proven that to respond in forensically corrective terms to *anything* can only be, at best, to pull at—and actually *tighten*—our collective representational chains?

As a first approximation, it is reasonable to label this the political dilemma of forensic criticism. It is an acute dilemma for me because my own politics, fully elaborated, put me in opposition not only to many actual images in the media but also to the very consolidation of media power that, by my own account, correcting those images only furthers. I do not promise extraction from this dilemma, nor redemption on this score for forensic criticism. It seems to me that if the assumption of the position of corrector has certain implications, then it has them. Grim as it sounds, part of this chapter's purpose is to introduce this insight, let it run its course, and survey the damage. I shall, however, battle my own pessimism at least to the extent of speculating on one escape route. We will come full circle to this and thereby to a second value for the term "political" as it pertains to forensic criticism. First, let us pursue the general mapping out and closer contemplation of the topic.

Let me circle back to an early point: no act of correcting, in the sense that I have developed the concept here, is exempt from the basic dilemma that characterizes the practice, namely, that the *very act* of condemning a film for having gotten something wrong implies that it might have gotten the thing right—which, in turn, implies that the *difference* between reality and representation is quantifiable, describable, and—given the right kind and degree of textual tinkering—reducible to zero.[20]

Politically radical corrective commentary about reactionary texts is not exempt. No corrective comment can earn exemption on the basis of anything. I have been clear about my anxiety in this matter, which is the anxiety associated with having logically demonstrated that *my* politics cannot be meaningfully expressed through the form. I do not know that I can alleviate this anxiety, but if there is an agenda to pursue in this connection, it does not consist of ranking corrective remarks according to their political enlightenment—a pointless exercise because, indifferent to such oblique categorization, they go on doing their work *as corrective remarks.* For this reason, among others, I offer as the substance of the political aspect of the practice something other than a measurement or note taking of the political tenor of corrective remarks.

The trajectory we have followed through the textual, topical, and ethical aspects of forensic criticism has taken us increasingly out of the realm of the corrector's cognitive processes and into the realm of publicness, shared discourse, and the triangulations that embrace the *addressee* of the corrective remark. Without leaving the corrector behind, we have moved gradually onto the more public stage. The political aspect, as I envision it, takes us to the next step in this progression. It is the most fully public and inclusive aspect of the practice. It is also the most abstract and complex (that is, composite), and it takes us to the limits of the argument. It might mean, in part (the part that might bear most strongly on the corrector's inner faculties), the decision to perform correction upon a text *in the knowledge of, and therefore despite, the futility of proposing an alternative text*—that is, casting rhetoric at a text because we can do nothing else, not because we are hopeful about the prospect of exactitude. More fully, and in the public sense that I wish to suggest, the political aspect might mean, or extend to, what its addressee thinks about a corrective remark, hears in it, chooses to do (or not do) about it. Indeed, the adjective "political," in this light, alludes not to a semantic property of the corrective remark (as in "This is/is not a very 'political' statement") but to a historical feature of the world of people and their discourses with which forensic criticism, by virtue of being a discourse of people, has full rights of intercommunication. In other words, it has to do with power. Forensic criticism, if political in this sense, may be an illogical enterprise (because hopeless); it may even be multiple enterprises—the spoken, the heard—rather than one with several aspects. Certainly, the question of what is done with it once it is public—what may be its power to affect, to enlighten, even to influence the topical registers of its respondents, not necessarily by direct argumentation but by the light of the sparks given off as it collides with the unsatisfactory text—points us (designedly, in terms of my argument) toward the least controllable, predictable, even visible part of the corrective remark's life cycle. The political aspect is highly speculative and ideal. It is, in fact, the expression, on my part, of the wish for an escape route—a way to establish the promise, if not the certainty, that forensic criticism might—*might*—have some purpose beyond the ethical promotion and moral intervention of its practitioner, even if that purpose never achieves parity with the practice's more troubling attributes of tenacity and power.

The political aspect of forensic criticism, then, does not refer to the political stance of any given remark but to its life at the farthest reaches beyond its initial and immediate material situation. I prefer not to spell out at any length what this might entail, but it could, imaginably, be a child overhearing an adult correctively protest an obnoxious racial image in, say, a Burger King commercial and carrying away from that experience the beginnings of a sensitivity to stereotypes for which a mild affirmation of the dreaded corrective paradox would be, in the overall scheme of things, a small price to pay. (In keeping with the project of *not* simply ranking corrective remarks by political content, moreover, we would have to speculate—although it is harder to flesh the speculation out—that even Sarris on checkout counters could have a political life in this sense.) In short, while I am convinced that the allowance of correction in the regime of cinema signifies, always and irreducibly, the impotence rather than the breadth of responsive power, I nonetheless believe that the whole regime—forensic criticism and all—can exist in a world in which other, forward-moving things are also possible.

If the political aspect of forensic criticism is its life beyond its immediate context, it is also its life beyond any certainty of retrieval. There is nothing untoward about this. In the end, it may be in the power of the rhetor—but may also be in the power of the respondent—to see to the reconsecration of rhetoric to something other than transparency.

Notes

1. W. Lance Bennett and Martha S. Feldman, *Reconstructing Reality in the Courtroom: Justice and Judgment in American Culture* (New Brunswick, N.J.: Rutgers University Press, 1981), 33.

2. Andrew Sarris, review of *Terms of Endearment,* in *Village Voice,* 13 December 1983, 71; reprinted in *Film Review Annual,* ed. Jerome S. Ozer (Englewood, N.J.: Film Review Publications, 1984), 1219–21. Subsequent references to the *Film Review Annual* will be given as "*FRA* (year), page."

3. Sheila Benson, review of *Yentl,* in *Los Angeles Times,* 18 November 1983, "Calendar," 1; reprinted in *FRA* (1984), 1431.

4. Robert Asahina, review of *Raiders of the Lost Ark,* in *New Leader,* 19 June 1981, 19; reprinted in *FRA* (1982), 975–76.

5. Philip Strick, review of *JFK,* in *Sight and Sound,* February 1992, 48; reprinted in *FRA* (1992), 703.

6. Jami Bernard, review of *Teenage Mutant Ninja Turtles,* in *New York Post,* 30 March 1990, 21; reprinted in *FRA* (1991), 1413.

7. John Coleman, review of *Silkwood,* in *New Statesman,* 13 April 1984, 29; reprinted in *FRA* (1984), 1069.

8. Review of *The Lonely Villa,* in *The New York Dramatic Mirror,* 61.1591 (19 June 1909), 16; reprinted in *Selected Film Criticism, 1896–1911,* ed. Anthony Slide (Metuchen, N.J.: Scarecrow Press, 1981), 64–65.

9. It is important to note that forensic criticism cuts a path across otherly defined questions of plot premise, suspension of disbelief, and verisimilitude. Consider not only the Mutant Turtles correction but the following comment by Jami Bernard on *Dream a Little Dream:* "Of course, the whole idea of a body-switch is, you know, to walk a mile in another man's shoes. But the old geezer in the young body mostly learns to mousse his hair like Michael Jackson and do a self-conscious moonwalk, while the irreverent teen does not enter Lobard's body at all (whaa?) but lounges around in the ozone basking in the thought of never going to school again" (*New York Post,* 3 March 1989, 27; reprinted in *FRA* [1990], 327).

10. For a treatment of the rhetoric of film interpretation in a more general sense, see David Bordwell, *Making Meaning: Inference and Rhetoric in the Interpretation of Cinema* (Cambridge, Mass.: Harvard University Press, 1989), esp. 34–40 and chaps. 9–10.

11. This and the following terms and descriptions (though not the examples) are taken verbatim from the alphabetical list in Richard A. Lanham, *A Handlist of Rhetorical Terms,* 2d ed. (Berkeley: University of California Press, 1991). This book is a wonderful starting place for scholars from any field who are interested in the diversity of rhetorical techniques and figures.

12. Stephen Harvey, review of *The Shining,* in *Saturday Review,* July 1980, 64; reprinted in *FRA* (1981), 861.

13. Sheila Benson, review of *Miller's Crossing,* in *Los Angeles Times,* 5 October 1990, "Calendar," 10; reprinted in *FRA* (1991), 1018.

14. John Coleman, review of *Yentl,* in *New Statesman,* 30 March 1984, 27; reprinted in *FRA* (1984), 1433.

15. Kenneth M. Chanko, review of *Blue Velvet*, in *Films in Review*, December 1986, 622; reprinted in *FRA* (1987), 145.

16. Bill Harris, from a transcription of a televised broadcast of "At the Movies," 17 January 1988 (emphasis added).

17. For a treatment of the language of reviews in its capacity as a rhetoric of persuading, in the sense of winning the reader over and/or influencing the reader to patronize or not, see Robert L. Root Jr., *The Rhetorics of Popular Culture* (New York: Greenwood Press, 1987), esp. chap. 6.

18. Tzevetan Todorov, *The Poetics of Prose*, trans. Richard Howard (Ithaca, N.Y.: Cornell University Press, 1977), 81, 80. For a lively look at rhetoric and Sicilian legal process, see Bromley Smith, "Corax and Probability," in *Readings in Rhetoric*, ed. Lionel Crocker and Paul A. Carmack (Springfield, Ill.: Charles C. Thomas, 1965), 38–67.

19. Sheila Benson, review of *Blow Out*, in *Los Angeles Times*, 24 July 1981, "Calendar," 1; reprinted in *FRA* (1981), 108.

20. This, in turn, suggests the question, "Are there ways to protest against imagery that are not corrective?" Probably. But since corrective discourse is so (frighteningly) widespread and deeply entrenched, it deserves to be talked about. In other words, I have taken a positive approach, dealing with something that in my view exists, whether or not other things that are not it also exist. I would add that what I consider the problem with forensic criticism—that is, its affirmation of the very narratorial power it appears to usurp—extends to many discourses.

Part 4

Power, Prison, Pain

8

Bound and Determined

The Streets of Manhattan

South of the numbered streets on the island of Manhattan, there remains a fair amount of island and a fair number of streets. But these streets do not obey a grid principle, like the ones to the north: they have names rather than numbers, and they twist and turn. This part of Manhattan is more like London than it is like the orderly numerical grid north of it. The only way to know these streets is to know them—not an external algorithm on the basis of which they or their internal relations can be inferred, but *them.*

This image of order bordering on disorder, or linearity bordering on nonlinearity, resonates in two different but, I would argue, very closely related ways with the matter of law in film. First, it evokes the transition to the far side of the verdict—that is, what happens after the stories have been told, the versions and verbalizations thrown into the procedural cauldron and distilled down to a single word. On the way *to* the verdict, things fall rather nicely into place. Detectives look for stories, audiences look for stories, the personnel of the courtroom look for and receive stories. Storytelling allows for large amounts of play at the cusps of event and word, film and word, event and film. The ripples of that play wash over history, pedagogy, film theory, and legal theory. The machinery behind all this is complex—and varyingly so—but purposeful. There is a telos, and the teleology is that of the verdict: a single word exerting gravity on all the other words, a word of institutional truth. The narrative may not be linear, but to the extent it is not, its nonlinearity can be measured only in relation to a familiar and anticipated line.

Then—after the verdict—come sentencing and *punishment*. Like the southern streets of Manhattan, legal punishment in films runs not only in unpredictable directions but unpredictably. Moreover, it does not lead anywhere, at least not axiomatically or obviously. Prison, the home of the criminally unclean, is a narrative tabula rasa; all teleological bets are off.

Second, the breakdown of the Manhattan grid suggests the entire matter of extrasystemic or multisystemic law—the presence and operation of systems of law that are not logomorphic systems, that are not traditional Anglo-American (or similar) systems, and that stand in opposition to those traditional systems. As Bennett and Feldman remind us, there is nothing inevitable about the grounding of any given legal system in the production of linear, probabilistic stories.[1] Similarly, nothing prevents a film about law from extending its reach beyond the representation of a logomorphic, narrative-based legal system. As it turns out, there are indeed some films (though not many) that very directly take on the matter of conflicting and incompatible legal *systems*—as opposed to, or in addition to, the matter of conflicting legal *stories* within one system. (I will examine two such films in detail.)

Making a supertopic of these two things—the representation of punishment and the clash between traditional and alternative legal models—may seem an awkward or unintuitive step. However, I see them as transformations of each other in important respects. The use of, say, sorcery as a principle of legal process has something in common with, say, escape from prison: both of these devices represent a challenge to or contravention of the linearity of "the" system and therefore have more in common with each other than either has with a run-of-the-mill guilty verdict in the courtroom (however complex the plot leading up to that verdict may have been).

"The" system coerces prisoners into prison. It also coerces those whose legal sensibilities lie outside the system into the system (and possibly into prison). Films about prison tend to be about the manipulation of restrictive space by prisoners: escape, smuggling in of drugs, and so forth. Such films represent personal (and occasionally political) wrestlings with the system. To that extent, when a film represents a sustained conflict between different legal or quasi-legal ideologies, such representation may be described at least formalistically as an extrapolation into the earlier phases of the process of the kind of system-oppositional practices that characterize many prison films.

In other words, I tend to interpret the representation of imprisonment as a special case of the representation of resistance to coercion into the system, the latter being something that can take numerous other forms. While this approach may be more rhetorical than historical (with regard to the relationships between films), it has the effect of grouping themes and theoretical issues together that do relate to each other at many levels. Another effect of clustering these lines of examination in one section is that Robert Cover's article "Violence and the Word" becomes and remains relevant to much of what will be under discussion here—arguably acceptable in itself as a reason to organize the material this way, given both the power of Cover's argument and the article's historical position as a watershed moment in the criticism of "law-and- . . ." schools of thought.[2]

Cover argues principally for a recognition of the unique, singular nature of judicial pronouncements. They are, he reminds us, not interpretive acts in any received sense of the term but, rather, acts that result in actual, physical actions against actual people:

> Legal interpretation takes place in a field of pain and death. This is true in several senses. Legal interpretive acts signal and occasion the imposition of violence upon others: A judge articulates her understanding of a text, and as a result, somebody loses his freedom, his property, his children, even his life. Interpretations in law also constitute justifications for violence which has already occurred or which is about to occur. When interpreters have finished their work, they frequently leave behind victims whose lives have been torn apart by these organized, social practices of violence. Neither legal interpretation nor the violence it occasions may be properly understood apart from one another. This much is obvious, though the growing literature that argues for the centrality of interpretive practices in law blithely ignores it.[3]

The literature to which Cover refers here is the work of legal scholars working from the perspective of law as interpretation and/or law as literature.[4] He argues that equating judicial language with interpretive language, or with literary texts awaiting literary interpretation, ignores the fact that pain and death and violence are singularities and that, in law, "great issues of constitutional interpretation that reflect fundamental questions of political allegiance . . . clearly carry the seeds of violence (pain and death) at least from the moment that the understanding of the political texts becomes embedded in the institutional capacity to take collective action. But it is precisely this embedding of an understanding of political text in institutional modes of action that distinguishes legal interpretation from the interpretation of literature, from political philosophy, and from constitutional criticism."[5]

I have already expressed a film theorist's concern, with respect to real-world stakes, over the weightiness of film theory as compared with that of even a law-as-literature approach. Cover's categorical distinction between interpretive acts and judicial pronouncements poses a yet greater challenge in the matter of interpreting film and specifically interpreting films about law. Film theorists operate at several levels of remove from pain and death and from the reality of the imposition of those things on human beings. In some respects, this is indeed a boundary of the argument. Film is never going to matter the way that courtroom sentencing matters. It is tempting to remind oneself of *The Thin Blue Line*, a film whose representation of the ambiguities of a real-life murder case resulted in public awareness of the case, an appeal, and the eventual pardon of the man who had been convicted of the murder. Still, it must be accepted that my engagement here with Cover is taking place somewhere on the way down from the zenith of his argument. I continue to maintain that film is important and that legal representation in film is important; and the issues that Cover asks legal scholars to grapple with remain in view, at least as issues, when it comes to film and the interpretation of law in film. But it would terribly disserve Cover's achievement to try to stage some kind of compromise with his argument—to reintroduce the analogies and points of comparison that he has demonstrated not to be analogies but radical differences. There is no gainsaying pain and death.

Filmic treatments of legal punishment, particularly imprisonment, may exhibit elective reflexivity and refraction; in fact, perhaps oddly, they tend almost always to do so. After all, a film that was really about people rotting away in prison, deprived of their narrative agency in any (to put it crudely) interesting sense, would not be interesting. Something has to happen.

Frequently, prison in films fails to stop people from doing what they do. Prisoners murder each other when and where they want to; mob bosses conduct business on the outside; drugs and weapons arrive on the scene as wanted or needed. While these activities of course serve the purpose of allowing there to be a plot, on closer inspection they are very banal, even for plot fodder: they rarely extend to anything but an uninteresting subset of what the same characters would be doing outside prison, and the real story becomes the processes by which they manage to maneuver around the guards or by which their cohorts manage to smuggle things to them. Relatively rarely, moreover, are even these feats strikingly ingenious; rather, they tend to take forms like lock-picking equipment delivered in a kiss or laundry service as a cover for communication. This is not to say that the representation of illicit activities in prisons tends to be any less drab than the representation of nonprison life in commercial fiction films but only that it stakes its narrative interest on *the process of circumvention,* whether ingenious or not.

"The violence of the act of sentencing," writes Cover, "is most obvious when observed from the defendant's perspective. Therefore, any account which seeks to downplay the violence or elevate the interpretive character or meaning of the event within a community of shared values will tend to ignore the prisoner or defendant and focus upon the judge and the judicial interpretive act."[6] This is not a plea for sentimentality or sympathy with the criminally culpable but rather a clarification of exactly the nature of the connections between the regimes of language and those of physical violence and restraint. As far as defendants are concerned, judges' words are violent; the notion that those words are actually literary or interpretive makes as little sense from the point of view of the defendant as it can ever make—which is to say, none.[7] Another way to put this is that the logomorphic and logoteleological aspects of judicial pronouncement are, at most, the end of one thing but, at least, the beginning of another.

A judge, then, puts an end to the defendant's story by imprisoning the defendant. Perhaps this is why numerous films about prison[8] involve a prisoner's recourse to acts of storytelling, narration, and authorship—diaries, tapes, confessions. In these circumstances, such authorial acts represent a kind of pseudojudicial gesture, an effort to remand the entire matter to the arena of narrative, story, and interpretation. This effort, moreover, is not an effort of the character portrayed in the film (as is nothing, strictly speaking) but an effort of textual organization and plot. It reasserts the principle that what is happening is the writing of a story—while that story takes place entirely on the far side of the actual verdict, in (but in friction with) the representation of legally mandated pain and death.[9]

In various ways, then, and to a surprising degree (given that the point of prison is to stop people from doing things), prisoners are in control of the story. This, in turn, is what makes the representation of imprisonment in film so open-ended and nonlinear: there is no single, almost-universal telos comparable to the verdict in the prepunishment phases of legal process. Even escape is not an inevitably operative goal, though it certainly looms large. The narrative fascination thus comes in large part from this disposition of things: the assignment of a role of agency and/or authorship to those who are bound and who by rights should be not determining but determined.

Up to the moment of the verdict, the story of the law progressively occludes the story of the accused (whether the accused be an innocent person falsely accused or a guilty person justly accused but unconfessing). After the verdict, in the geometry of punishment, the tables are turned: the prisoner's story—not the past, but the story now under construction *by the prisoner*—becomes central. Even the effort involved in *having* a story becomes central.

In this respect, films that represent prison exhibit a significant degree of elective reflexivity. Rarely cut entirely adrift from the story of crime and sentencing,[10] the portrayal of prison nonetheless takes us automatically beyond those elements. Any attempt on the part of a prisoner to write the story, to define the struggle as a struggle of narrative(s), constitutes at least a minor elaboration (and possibly a major one) of the issues of determinism and reflexivity that transect law in film generally. Whether or not such films are refractive, in the sense that I have used the term, is another matter.

The Double Bind: Law and Film beyond the Logomorph

As in the case of courtroom representation, I do not want to linger long on a genre-ish study of prison representation. Rather, having introduced the issue of postverdict narrativity, I want to generalize back from it, as promised, to the matter of narrative coercion. By this I mean, simultaneously, narratives about coercion; the coercion of narrative, its constraint, as a function of legal power; and the coercion of incongruent systems or codes of law into the narrative, logomorphic mold.

Cover directly addresses the matter of the difference between and among legal systems, not just as a matter of what goes on in court, nor just as a matter of what happens after the verdict, but looking at the system, irreducibly, as encompassing both. Particularly striking is his analysis of *United States v. Tiede*, a 1979 case in which Judge Herbert Stern, presiding over the United States Court for Berlin, was responsible for sentencing a convicted skyjacker. The complexity of the case, Cover argues (acknowledging Stern's own "unusually lucid appreciation" of what was at stake), had to do very concretely with "the significance of the institutional connections between the judicial word and the violent deeds it authorizes."[11] Writes Cover:

> After a jury trial, opposed by the prosecution, and a verdict of guilty on one of the charges, Stern was required to perform the "simple" interpretive act of imposing the appropriate sentence. As a matter of interpreting the governing materials on sentencing it might indeed have been a "simple" act— one in which relatively unambiguous German law was relatively unambiguously to be applied by virtue of American law governing a court of occupation.
>
> Stern brilliantly illuminated the defects in such a chain of reasoning. The judicial interpretive act in sentencing issues in a deed—the actual performance of the violence of punishment upon a defendant. But these two— judicial word and punitive deed—are connected only by the social cooperation of many others, who in their roles as lawyers, police, jailers, wardens, and magistrates perform the deeds which judicial words authorize. Cooperation among these officials is usually simply assumed to be present, but, of course, the conditions which normally ensure the success of this cooperation may fail in a variety of ways.[12]

Recognizing the unacceptability of simply cutting and pasting what would have been the appropriate sentence, had the case *and its legal host environment* been domestic, Stern sentenced the defendant to time served—that is, he freed him.[13]

This extraordinary tale from the annals of international law holds a lesson for any study or contemplation of the matter of one legal system coming into contact, or conflict, with another—that lesson being, in the main, that there is no "the" system, such that it accounts for everything and covers, with anything remotely resembling justice, all situations and eventualities. To explore these themes in connection with law in film, I will look in some detail at two films, both of whose stories revolve around the friction and incompatibility between logomorphic systems of law and other systems: *A Question of Silence*, by Marleen Gorris, and *The Last Wave*, by Peter Weir.

These two films make for an interesting pair, inasmuch as there are noteworthy parallels between them. Both involve a professional expert (psychiatrist, lawyer) engaged on a murder case whose multiple defendants are members of a marginalized and misunderstood group (women, Aborigines). In both cases, guilt in legal-propositional terms is not difficult to establish, if it is even in doubt. In both films, although to different effect, the professional is drawn to and into the intersystemic conflict and, gradually coming to an awareness of the difference between the premises of his or her profession and those of the legal system of the outsiders, undergoes an empathetic and identificatory process of change, induction, and conscience. Finally, language and verbal representation are pitted in both against a series of oppositionally polarized terms and phenomena—magic, silence, pictorial representation and symbolism, metamorphosis, water, dream.

I approach these films not specifically as prison films (though both include prison sequences, rather lengthy ones in the case of *A Question of Silence*) nor specifically for their resonances with the story of Judge Stern. Rather, I view them as casting a net that catches up these issues, not in the form of a checklist of themes or plot elements, but in ways that intricately represent and explore the difficulties—the anguish—at the cusp between systems of law, doing so specifically through the instrument of narrative film. It turns out, as I hope to demonstrate, that narrative film provides some cusps and margins of its own, powerfully suited to the representation of encounters between logomorphic regimes and those whose substance and structure lie outside the word.

Second-Degree Murder: The Synoptist Holds Her Tongue

Legal process, I have argued, revolves around the aggregation of second-degree narratives—retellings, testimony, versions—and their gradual reconciliation into a relatively frozen and theoretically accurate master narrative. Filmic comprehension, I have also suggested, does something rather similar. If we are going to cast the net outside the regime(s) of telling, retelling, verbalizing, and narrative reconciliation, we can do little better than to look closely at the matter of *silence*—the opposite, the antiprinciple of logomorphic and propositional constitution of reality.

As a narrative and/or reflexive strategy, silence has some near relatives: that is, legal logomorphic—the ritualistic use of narrative language to gain purchase on irreducibly absent referent events—may be troubleshot and probed through a variety of cinematic devices. Often, the reckoning with these concerns is conducted by means of the critical juxtaposition of filmically enacted and judicially narrated versions of events—activity, in other words, at the cusp between word and film. This play at the cusp of representation is not only overdetermined (since the verbalizing impulse is itself a datum of the story, which is filmic but is a story by virtue of its logomorphism, and so forth) but ironic. Its irony can take many forms, depending on exactly how the verbal approach to representation in the courtroom is positioned with respect to the filmic sequences with which it shares narrative space. Often, it is a question of information available to the audience, courtesy of filmic representation or flashback, but not to the court. This is the case, for example, of the perfunctory injustice of *I Am a Fugitive from a Chain Gang* and *Sullivan's Travels*, films whose heroes' travails, known only to the audience, set them up as victims of an unknowing and uncaring legal system. Among their other points of connection, both of these films depict the brief processing of a hero/victim through a confidently narrating but ironically misinformed judiciary. The comic courtroom scene at the end of *What's Up, Doc?* illustrates a different configuration of disjuncture between what the audience has witnessed and what is available as narrative to the court, where in a very material and vivid way a multiplicity of voices vie for the role of veracious synoptist and provide an agitated assortment of conflicting versions. This particular courtroom, moreover, explores the irony of an indexical relationship between the filmically represented events leading up to the courtroom scene and their verbal synopsis during it: the verbal activity, that is, registers and repeats the hectic, exhilarated, chaotic properties of the neo-screwball text that it crowns.

The exploration of the mismatch between verbal and filmic representations may be undertaken according to any plan affecting audience knowledge, metanarrative coaxing, and narrational ordering. A case like *I Confess* flirts with an injustice related to that carried out in the two prison camp/courtroom films mentioned earlier but with a significantly different economy of audience and character knowledge and narrative privilege (who has the narrative, what the narrative really is, etc.). In *Witness for the Prosecution*, the strands of the multiply twisted revelations are only sorted out *after* the law has finished with its narrative; the (first-time) audience has actually been shown a great deal but does not know it.[14] The irony of the failure of legal narrative as conduit of the referent event is therefore at least partially withheld until a very late point in the film, and here the question of the relation between verbal and filmic versions becomes almost inextricably gnarled.

Understood in the context of a variety of permutations of the balance between filmic (i.e., audience-available) and legal narrativity, silence in the courtroom always carries some reflexive weight because it represents the extreme of one of the two terms of the equation. (The other term is of course variable; the silence of a witness or defendant does not have to be balanced by lengthy or richly detailed enactments or flashbacks—although such balancing certainly enhances the irony and drama of the silence.) Silence, like speech, has a context from which it gains meaning. *I Confess* involves not absolute silence but the refusal to say certain things, and the consequent consolidation of power by the law. During his encounter with the justice system, Sullivan can speak only from an amnesiac and aphasic state in which he is unable to match even superficially the articulatory and narrative power wielded against him.

In addition to its position in, or partial determination of, various imperfect discourses, silence in the courtroom can signal an arrival at a point qualitatively beyond the irony of failing to find a correct match between verbal and filmic representations or to bring both into accord with a third term—a narrative referent—to which both are subservient. Silence in the filmic courtroom can also add something new: the uncanny possibility of complete escape from verbal recountability, from narrative, and perhaps from narrativity.

One remarkable example of this potential, as of so many others, is *Vertigo,* if we accept that film's tribunal scene as courtroom representation.[15] The investigator at the tribunal tells—half with words, half with raised eyebrows—a satisfactorily crafted story of Scottie's irresponsibility and culpability in the death of Madeleine Elster. Given what the audience knows (or thinks it knows), this verbal synopsis, entered into the legal record, serves only to indict itself *and verbal narrative in general* and to ratify the status of the film as something beyond words, something not only more expressive than a verbal account but even more accurate (however measured). Words come out looking bad, not only because they are mere words, but because they get everything wrong anyway—everything that they might have gotten right, which may not have been much. Scottie's silence in response to this outrage against his character is of course not the martyrdom of *I Confess,* with its Christological pathos (*"Mein Jesus schweigt zu falschen Lügen stille,"* says the text of Bach's *Saint Matthew Passion*), but a vast and echoless space into which words drop powerlessly. No longer is a battle of verbal terms waged over a filmically represented narrative prize. In the complete silence of *Vertigo* there is no protest nor even inarticulateness, only the mad and melancholy courtesy of standing to one side to give language room to pass by.

In *A Question of Silence,* the encounter between supplicants for and providers of plausible verbal narrative precedes the courtroom scene itself and constitutes a principal theme of the entire film. Psychiatrist Janine van den Bos is appointed to determine the mental conditions of three women on trial for the murder of a male boutique owner at his shop during business hours, a murder whose most recoverable features for the law are spontaneity, randomness, sadism, and irrationality. The eventual courtroom scene revolves mainly around Janine's presentation of her controversial finding that the women are sane.

In addition to being a film about silence, *A Question of Silence* is also a film about verbal synopsis and narrative secondarization. I posit this not strictly because it is a courtroom film and I have posited as much about all courtroom films, but because this particular film is explicitly concerned throughout with the proliferation and comparison of versions, problems of metanarrative and plausibility, mechanical reproduction of the voice and body, repetition, interrogation, narrative correcting, doubting, seeing, and telling.

These themes are explored extensively through the mechanism of juxtaposing filmic enactments and verbal recountings of events. Enacted sequences dovetail into later—now present—verbal reports (we see Janine interview Annie but hear Annie's response as it is repeated by Janine to her husband at their home). Janine's tape recorder connects representations of noncontiguous spaces and times. Also, the film has a complex network of flashbacks, with episodes or images culled from numerous nodes of past and present time:

1. the main present time of the story;
2. the murder in the boutique (shown over multiple flashback sequences);
3. Andrea at a board meeting at work;
4. Christina with her family, as her husband goes off to work;
5. Annie after the murder;
6. Andrea after the murder;
7. Christina after the murder;
8. Christina sitting in her living room (imagined by/imaged through Janine);
9. Annie with her family (imagined by Annie after the murder).

Even this rough enumeration (which bulldozes over many subtle points of subjectivism and mental perspective) suggests that the film's sequences are very miscellaneous in their distribution about fictional space and time. Some of them are contiguous as between each other but broken across the film (the murder, Annie after the murder). Some are simultaneous and broken across the film (the three women after the murder); or projected into indeterminate past or even imaginary time by present or already analeptic characters (the subjective or projected images of Christina and Annie in their homes); and so forth.

The significant point about these filmic wanderings around space and time, and what defines their position in an atmosphere of crisis for second-degree narrative and synopsis, is that they always occur in counterpoint and thematically open tension with verbalization and recountability. Some of them follow on or displace verbal narratives in a more or less classical way—that is, someone starts talking about the past and, after a certain amount of speech, the film takes over with a flashback. Others are not triggered by any obviously connected present-time narrating act—indeed, one of them, Christina's ride with her child on the Ferris wheel after the murder, emphatically can have no corresponding diegetic verbal instance, since Christina herself does not speak. Throughout the film, the registers of verbal and visual narrative rub and clash against each other, and the very frequency and variety with which they do so brings the troubled relation between filmic enactment and verbal synopsis to the fore well before the courtroom scene takes place.

This constant friction and mutual superimposition of verbalized and filmically enacted sequences constitutes one facet of an even more global theme in the film: namely, the opposition, at many levels and in many contexts, between, first, verbal discourse and the institutions that serve and are served by it and, second, what might at this level of generality (and for lack of a better word) be called nonverbal or extraverbal experience. This opposition, generally, is polarized along lines of sexual difference—somewhat in congruence with the Lacanian realms of the symbolic and imaginary.[16] The prolific and power-wielding discourses of the language-centered, male-dominated professions (psychiatry, law, business, medicine) stand in opposition to those experiences, and in some cases discourses, that come to be associated with both the lives of women and their desire for change: dream, silence, nonverbal intimacy, drawing, and laughter.

Film itself occupies an ambivalent position. It is of course employed as the transcendent vehicle of the expression of the polarity itself; and where verbalization per se comes under attack, it is filmic representation of one kind or another that gainsays it. But film is not entirely absolved of association with the abusers of either narrative or judicial power—as suggested most vividly by the prison scene in which multiple video monitors track Janine, the prisoners, and the wardens walking from cell to cell between interviews. By the same token, the film does not advocate anti-intellectualism or inarticulateness as a response to the inequities of linguistic power; that is, language is not so irrevocably male that it cannot be participated in by women.

The central motif in conjunction with which this opposition comes to expression is Janine's growing awareness of the ambivalent nature of her own work and its larger ideological context. She undergoes a kind of induction into the nonverbal and a concomitant refeminization of her conscientious but mechanized professionalism. Beginning as a highly successful psychiatrist, with extensive experience and reputation in her field, she gradually develops the faculties for understanding the implications of her work and its irreducibly oppositional relation to the actual situation of the three women who become her clients. Prior to the courtroom sequence, this transformative and educational process culminates along several of its trajectories in what might be roughly described as an initiation scene between Janine and Andrea—a scene that speaks (or, more to the point, does not speak) for itself by the very fact that no one, of either sex, is really able to categorize it or even recount it confidently.[17]

For Janine, the case of the three women is, as she says, more than just another case. Beyond the argumentation of Andrea and the verbosity of Annie lies the silence of Christina, and it is, above all, this latter enigma that Janine must not only reconcile herself to as a matter of professional procedure (where speech and narrative are the norms) but accommodate psychically and morally, even at the cost of reconsidering the claim of her profession to frictionless proximity with legal process.[18]

Christina speaks exactly once in the film, asking Janine to remind her husband about an appointment with their son's teacher. Before and after that, until her first outburst of laughter in the courtroom, she is silent—not aphasic, logophobic, or rude, but silent. Moreover, hers is a silence on the cusp of two silences: a place of exile and a position of resolve. Understood within psychiatry as catatonia, Christina's silence is interpreted by Andrea as the product of will: "She stopped talking because no one was listening." Relegated to silence as a token of her subordination to men, and continually rechoosing it over language,

Christina lives out an endless and irreducible spiral of bivalence, availing herself of and suffering by one and the same weapon.[19]

Silence does not resolve itself here into speech (as it does, for example, in *Judgment at Nuremberg*) but rather into laughter—which takes us to the courtroom scene.

It is of great importance in this film that the debate in court is not over the guilt or innocence of the defendants but over their sanity. The issue of sanity intersects with the practice of producing cogent and plausible narrative in a particular, acute way; indeed, sanity is measured as a function of the effects of narrative and the ability of language to contain action and thought. By approaching the crime this way, the film actually cuts through more effectively to the stakes of verbalization, linguistic representation, and power than might have been the case had the premise involved the empirical question of culpability.

Newly aware of her own position, Janine initially tries to do battle in court by the rules of the game of judicial process—that is, to explain and defend her position in articulate and professional language. When she first reveals her finding that the defendants are sane, the spectators in the courtroom become noisy and the judge demands silence—a demand not ostensibly targeted at Janine yet perhaps not meaninglessly juxtaposed to her pronouncement, as if her audacity had warranted a retaliatory recapturing of the territory of logic and rationality from the women.

An admonition from the judge to Janine that her report will be of great importance to the outcome of the case provokes the scene's first laughter, an isolated outburst from Christina. In her subsequent presentation, Janine attempts to harmonize her professional skill with the turbulent conditions of the current case, but this effort breaks down precisely at a point where she and the prosecutor have presented each other with irreconcilable assertions—more than irreconcilable; they are mutually incomprehensible. Janine has identified gender difference as the central issue, while the prosecutor has announced his belief that the case would be no different if it had involved a group of men who had murdered a female shop owner.

The prosecutor acts in this sequence as vehement and polemical rhetor and synoptist, vividly describing the crime and appealing to the obviousness of its insane nature. For the audience, meanwhile, this is hardly the first "version" of the murder—verbal or filmic. We have seen in it flashbacks (its more gruesome particulars kept below the bottom of the frame, while the camera registers the unhurried violence of the women, wielding weapons from above). We have also heard it described by the doctor who performed the autopsy, to some extent by Annie and Andrea, and by the court clerk in reading the charges against the defendants.

From the point of view of activity at the verbal/filmic border, the relation of the flashbacks to the prosecutor's speeches invites our closest attention among these instances. Importantly, there is nothing in the flashbacks that contradicts the prosecutor's characterizations of the act (it does not turn out, for example, that the women were actually defending themselves from an immediate physical danger). To point this out is not to shrink from or attempt to dilute the impact of the film but to open the door onto its most provocative area. Here we are in the realm of conflicting versions but also of the underpinnings of narrative activity— that is, the linkages among narration, the inference of the nature of events, and legal power. This film is concerned with sanity among three murderers, the relation of mind to act. The filmic enactments of the crime are not simply pitted detail for detail against the prosecutor's verbal account; this is not *I Am a Fugitive from a Chain Gang.* Nor is the logomorphic teleology of the law simply transferred whole to the debate over sanity; that is, the flashbacks themselves are not conclusive metanarrative or authoritarian pronouncements on this issue either.

It is in this discrepancy of logical level that the prosecutor and Janine pass each other by. The prosecutor is concerned to tell a story and to draw what are for the law its obvious implications. Janine speaks from a position that is already concerned with gender, power, and oppression not as invisible premises, but as terms of meaning available to discourse and imagination; therefore, emphasizing as she does that the crime involved an attack by women on a male shop owner, she speaks what for the law can only be a language of riddles. Furthermore, Janine is the only woman who speaks in court at all. Despite her credentials and evidence, the law cannot accept Janine's opinion: sanity, after all, means the containment of women, and these women, having committed this murder, must therefore be insane.

The prosecutor's assertion that gender is irrelevant to the case must therefore be sublimely ludicrous. Immediately following the prosecutor's assertion of the irrelevance of sexual difference to the case, Annie breaks out laughing, and laughter quickly spreads through the group of defendants, Janine, and another group of four women—these being the four eyewitnesses to the murder. Like silence, the women's laughter is both a familiar element excerpted from the flow of articulate language and an oppositional practice sui generis, neither simply a reaction to the prosecutor's most recent remark nor a permanent surrender of the verbal. Indeed, laughter breaks forth when neither narrative *nor silence* is any longer worth the trouble of its own production. The law has blockaded the movement of verbal accounting in all directions long before any one voice might have harmonized the substance of the crime with the grammar of the law; and laughter, a kind of metasilence, emanates from a level yet further removed from even the possibility of representation, rebuttal, or defense in verbal terms.

The presence of the four witnesses at the boutique is the focal point of a crucial nexus of verbal/filmic relationships of narrative versions. Both Andrea and Annie conceal the truth about the witnesses from Janine, Andrea claiming that the boutique was empty during the crime, Annie that it was crowded like a market on Saturday. This presentation of multiple mendacious versions is a strikingly textbook case of contradiction and metanarrative, at least on the surface: the two women report different things, the flashbacks correct them. What contravenes the banality of this film/word narrative contest is the disappearance of the trail marked by this question into a space of *silence.* Janine's difficulties in learning the truth about the witnesses seem to point toward a resolution, the acquisition of a new, reconciling and correcting version to replace those she already has. But Janine never exactly learns the truth about this matter, in any form that could be registered as a datum of her professional investigation—that is, a story, an account. She notices the four witnesses in the courtroom, and later they appear on the steps outside the courthouse where Janine already stands. The film's final shot is a freeze-frame of Janine looking up at the four women who have stopped and look back at her. The resolution, for Janine, is beyond narrative and even beyond laughter; when she reaches this point, she simply looks.

The four witnesses do not speak and are virtually invisible to the law, whereas, not speaking and never mentioned, they are known *only* visually to the audience of the film until they laugh. They are not associated with the bringing to trial of the defendants; indeed, the process by which the crime was solved is accounted for in a rather perfunctory montage of testimony, all given by men. The four witnesses make themselves conspicuous in the courtroom—gathering around the stairwell in the middle of the room as the defendants are led away for a break, as well as joining in the laughter and being escorted out of the building—but the law, having investigated them out of existence, takes no notice.

They might have been synoptists, purveyors of narrative in the second degree, but they refuse that role, and the significance of that refusal for the film goes beyond its effect on the economy of power in the courtroom. The silence of the witnesses, in fact, does not seem to add anything to either side of the legal case nor to take anything away: the women were tracked down without (apparently) any help from the witnesses, and the two of them who speak about what they did in the boutique are very forthcoming. The silence of the witnesses is a relational term, an act invisible to the court but integral to the film-court-audience triangulation. Random in their very four-ness (not none, not a crowd), the witnesses are logically uninferable and undiscoverable to the law. They do not bargain for their silence but simply never make an offer of their voices, performing not so much a refusal to share information as a challenge to the very narratability of the event, a choice to preserve rather than donate for sacrifice the identity of the act only with itself.

Cataclysm and the Word

This examination of *A Question of Silence* has raised some questions about the status of film itself in the face of a filmic exploration of the relation between verbal and nonverbal—or logomorphic and nonlogomorphic—systems of interpretation. The medium of film, obviously, is called on to represent not only the polarization of systems but also the various phenomena belonging to both sides of it. The constitution of a verbal story is itself a datum of a filmic story, while that filmic story owes its own status as story, its narrativity, to its logomorphism, its preparedness to be understood as narrative. At one level this is self-evident. At another level, it opens onto the rather significant possibility of an irreducible paradox in a narrative film that undertakes to criticize the *judicial* process of the narrative representation of events, given that *filmic* representation (as argued here) relies on the word-based process of the generation of the logomorph for its own narrativity. In other words, we need to ask whether a film that is critical of the reliance of judicial process on verbal synopsis thereby pits filmic representation against verbal recounting—that is, whether it offers film as an instrument capable of representing the nonverbal, the nonpropositional—at the same time that it depends on verbal recountability for its own salvation from incoherence.

I would like to take up these points in connection with *The Last Wave*. As indicated earlier, this film bears some intriguing resemblances to *A Question of Silence*. In *The Last Wave*, a white lawyer is called on to defend a group of murder suspects—specifically, tribal Aborigines living in Sydney, Australia (while officialdom insists that there are no such people in the city). The murder, conducted through a quasimagical ritual (a tribal elder, sitting in a car, points a lethal object at the victim, whom he never touches), was an administration of punishment to a tribal man who had seen things—literally, objects—that he was not supposed to see.

David Burton, the lawyer, gradually finds himself drawn into the mythology of the group, turning out to have a spiritual and apparently genetic link to important mythological figures. The plot tends toward the magical and mystical and diverges in this respect from *A Question of Silence*; but, like the latter, it explores in considerable depth the clashing of systems, the underlying incompatibilities between, in this case, Anglo-Australian law and at least one version of tribal jurisprudence.

To be sure, narrative film can take a critical stance toward verbal recountability, among other ways by working to obscure its own narrative, by putting obstacles in the way of the crystallization of the logomorph itself. The initiation scene in *A Question of Silence* provided an example of this, a case where the film's thematic travel beyond language and verbalization coincides with a moment in the film that tends to baffle recounters and commentators. In this connection it is important to recall that the theory of the logomorph is not a theory of what films are or what they can contain but rather of how they achieve narrativity and how that narrativity allows them to circulate outside their own materiality. However speculative, this is sharply distinct from any claim (doomed to collapse) that filmic representation wants for nonlinguistic aspects. A film's thematic or subliminal resistance to verbal recountability cannot include a banishment of language from the texture of film but can constitute a kind of counterassertion of the nonlinguistic, regrouped outside logomorphic traversal and therefore on the fringes of narrativity itself. Thus, film may tamper with its own logomorphism, if it is willing to risk its own narrativity.

Language itself is further polarized in *The Last Wave*, particularly as between the rationalism of Western law and religion and the mysterious speech of the tribal elder Charlie. "Why didn't you tell me there were mysteries?" David asks of his stepfather, a minister. "David, my whole life has been about a mystery," is the reply. "No," objects David. "You stood in that church and explained them away." By contrast, the language of Charlie is prophetic, incantatory, and disintegrative. When David tracks Charlie down after learning that Charlie had been watching his house and family during his absence, he confronts him with the question, "Who are you?" Charlie takes up the question and repeats it over and over, turning David's troubled and confrontational language around and into a means of spiritual inquiry into David's position in the mysteries at hand—in fact, into David's identity. The scene ends as Charlie rises and walks away saying, "Don't speak in that court."

The theory of the logomorph—that is, of the word-shaped negotiation of narrative texts in any medium—is a theory of cataclysm, because texts are cataclysmic. Without the correct cognitive and institutional instruments, texts offer only fragments, shards, and the ruins of signification. Logomorphism is the counterdrive to cataclysm, the making sense of syncresis. To say that filmic spectators logomorphically negotiate a film is to theorize that they—we—deal with the sensory miscellany (light, colors, sounds) by packaging its elements into words or word-shaped mental constructs. Logomorphism is thus a drive toward containment and away from cataclysm.

The Last Wave, as it happens, is both a film about law and a film about cataclysm, a graphically and thematically cataclysmic text. The chief vehicle of cataclysm is water, which in various forms constantly intrudes and erupts into the film. In an early scene, somewhat reminiscent of *The Birds*, a group of schoolchildren seeks refuge in their classroom from a violent and unseasonal storm that issues first in rain and then in enormous chunks of hail, pounding on the roof and smashing the windows. Rain pours down virtually throughout the film. The first scene at David's home involves an ominous dripping, later a torrent, which is traced to an overflowing tub. Pedestrians float through floodwaters in front of David's windshield—a visual figure that, unlike the bathwater, is never absorbed into a rational framework. When David is finally given access to the underground sacred space of the tribal Aborigines, the painted images of prophecies he encounters culminate in great waves.

Water, the chief instrument of cataclysm in the film, encroaches on and pushes back the countertide of language, an opposition set up initially by the scene in the schoolroom—a place of learning and social-ization into the rational, violently and inexplicably disrupted by water. David tries to incorporate an understanding of the mystical tide into his own growing narration of the unexplained processes of which he seems to be becoming a part ("Your secret is linked to water," he says to Chris, the one among the defendants who is somewhat conflicted and forth-coming about the difficulties of reconciling tribal and mainstream le-gal processes), a reconciliation of cataclysm with discourse that is finally turned on its head in the courtroom scene. The oppositional relation between water and language is perhaps best captured in a scene in which Chris has come to dinner at the home of David and his wife, Annie, and has brought the silent Charlie with him. David offers Charlie a drink, and Chris responds, "He doesn't speak English. Water will be fine."

Water is a sort of alternative visual language for the film, something that can be referred to verbally but still asserts itself as if on behalf of the cataclysmic nature of the text against its logomorphic appropria-tion. The film plays with ambiguity and narrative obscurity (Are these images of water to be understood as visions? dreams? actual percepts?) but also pushes cataclysm, verbal recountability, and the relation be-tween narrative and event into the thematic foreground.

The final images of the film are of David entering water and then just of water. Exactly what is represented in this final cataclysm escapes renarration. If this claim seems to signal a veering toward a theory of immanent meaning in images (such-and-such is inherently less narra-tive than something else), I would hope to correct that impression by suggesting that the images at the end of *The Last Wave* could have been, historically, chosen to represent anything; that is, a screen full of water, of indeterminate scale and direction, might have been selected at some point in the history of filmic narrative to mean, "And now, a quasi-hallucinatory prolepsis"; or, "Meanwhile, back at the ranch." It is important not to relativize away the possibility of alternatives and counterfluxes. To say that the end of the film escapes renarration means that it mounts a cataclysmic attack on logomorphism and recount-ability—an attack that takes on value only to the extent that it is per-formed in response and relation to familiar or anticipated practices but is no less significant for having to be defined in relative terms. A film's putting baffles in the way of the logomorph must be understood as an approximate practice, occasional, conventional—certainly not under the complete and permanent control of the filmmaker; but, for all that, it can happen.

This thematic occupation with water and cataclysm thus falls largely into the category of the antilogomorphic filmic narrative, with all the tensions and paradox that entails. We may turn now to the highly and elaborately ironic courtroom scene in which the handling of the matter of verbal recountability changes the position of the terms of cataclysm and containment, putting at the film's disposal new and pointed ways of approaching them.

Two witnesses testify in this sequence. The first is the doctor who performed the autopsy on the victim. In conflict with an earlier report, he claims in court to have determined with certainty that the victim drowned—having been knocked down into a puddle on a sidewalk during a fight with the defendants. Earlier in the film, the doctor had been extremely uncertain of the cause of death. His tone on the witness stand suggests that his findings represent a decision to opt for professional dignity by gravitating, in the absence of a fully supportable position, toward the nearest available rational verbal explanation. The murder itself, moreover, had been enacted in the film, and it was made clear (insofar as clarity is one of the film's strategies) that it had involved tribal magic—specifically, the pointing of a lethal magical object at the victim, with no physical assault. Having reached a near certainty of his own on this point, David confronts the doctor with the sorcery scenario. The perfunctory reply is, "The deceased was not a tribal man."

The second witness is Chris, the young defendant with whom, throughout the film, David has the greatest amount of contact in both the physical and dream worlds. Chris having taken the courtroom oath, hand on Bible, David uses the power of the court as dangerous supplicant for narrative to wrest from Chris the admission that there are indeed tribal Aborigines in the city and that Chris and the other defendants are among them. At this juncture, however, David's own odyssey into tribal practices and mysteries comes too close to the logocentrism of Western law, and its bluff is called. Increasingly animated, and over objections from the prosecutor, David tries to draw Chris out on the reasons for the murder under tribal law:

> David: Did he see things? Did he touch things, steal something?
> Chris: Yes.
> David: What? Stones? These stones? Are these stones sacred? Chris, what is the secret Billy died for? Does someone forbid you to say? The one

who pointed the bone? The spirit man? Does he not want us to know
about the rain? Chris, tell them about the rain!
Chris: You're saying that! No more stones, no more secret things our fa-
thers did. You think it still happens? No. You got me mixed up. It was a
long time ago. We got drunk, had a fight, and that's all.

As in *A Question of Silence,* there is more going on in this filmic
courtroom than just a battle over correct and incorrect versions, more
than competition among narrative terms. At a certain level, of course,
David is right and Chris is lying. But to leave it at that does not do justice, so to speak, to the complexity of the scene. Consequent upon the
doctor's taking refuge in an elegant but uncertain medical narration of
the death, Chris may seek refuge in the doctor's testimony—which,
coming from an expert under oath, now represents an indelible node of
narratedness, an authorized and therefore resilient version. By denying
David's explanation and embracing the doctor's, Chris, like Janine,
manipulates not just symbols but entire symbolic processes and puts
the ball of verbal representation back in the court's court.

David's version of the murder is thereby turned against itself, and the
power of the courtroom is expropriated by the tribal narrator. Its very
accession to the status of courtroom narrative version puts the nonra-
tionalistic explanation of the murder into an arena where it can be re-
pudiated—and remystified. The only evidence it might have left would
surface as language, and as language it can easily be put in disadvanta-
geous narrative light: Western legal processes have little use for stories
about people dying because magical objects are pointed at them. In turn,
this protects the tribal system from becoming too public or too evident—an aspect of the plot to which Chris's character is central, as he
struggles with his dual roles as tribal man and legal client.

The most accessible thing logomorphically in *The Last Wave* is, in
some respects, the murder. It is enacted filmically, and there is available in court a nonconflicting verbal version of it. Along this trajectory,
the film is in a sense carefully unobscure. Thus, when the various versions of the murder blossom in the narrative garden of the courtroom,
the irony is not one of nonnarrativity (since the mystery is "solved")
but rather lies in the uses to which narrative is put and in the discrepancy between the availability of narrative and what is done with it. It
is not narrative per se that is pitted against the mysteries of tribal culture but narrative as a subsumptive instrument of veracity, and as guarantor of the eventual rectitude of the law.

Water, apocalypse, fulfillment—cataclysm presses in on all sides. David stands in the sacred space and utters *words* as he looks at the pictures, a final and reflexive act of containment: "A wave . . . a second wave . . ." But when the prophecy is fulfilled, it is in cataclysm and water: a last image, a last wave, just—but only just—on the other side of the last word.

Notes

1. W. Lance Bennett and Martha S. Feldman, *Reconstructing Reality in the Courtroom: Justice and Judgment in American Culture* (New Brunswick, N.J.: Rutgers University Press, 1981), esp. chap. 2.

2. Robert Cover, "Violence and the Word," *Yale Law Journal* 95 (1995): 1601–28.

3. Ibid., 1601.

4. Cover cites several examples of the kinds of work he means, including special issues of law journals devoted to these approaches (1601n2).

5. Ibid., 1606.

6. Ibid., 1608.

7. I leave aside the facile and, I would guess, unlikely case of a literary theorist on trial taking academic interest in his or her own sentencing.

8. I am deliberately avoiding the term "prison films," which conjures up too strongly a relatively narrow genre.

9. It seems to me, too, that many prisoners in films are involved in actual textual productivity: the memoirs of *Kind Hearts and Coronets*, the tape recorder of *In the Name of the Father*, various intra–prison cell recountings of crimes, claims of innocence, and so forth.

10. Here my avoidance of the term "prison films" comes into play: that term evokes, for me at least, a film whose running time is devoted almost entirely to scenes in prison, whereas a "film that represents prison" might actually devote more time to the portrayal of criminal acts, trials, postescape escapades, and so forth.

11. Cover, 1619.

12. Ibid., 1620.

13. It is interesting to consider this story and the points Cover makes in the course of telling it in relation to *In a Lonely Place*—specifically, the matter of Brub Nicolai and his malleability by "superiors." Lockner's regime of power would mean little if there were no Nicolai to embody his will, and Brub's compliance with Dixon's "orders" in the near-strangulation scene at Nicolai's house illustrates the further dangers of splicing the command-giver from one regime onto the underling from another.

14. This gloss on *Witness for the Prosecution* somewhat generously assumes that we are not supposed to recognize Dietrich in her Cockney guise.

15. I have no reservations about doing so. Far fewer courtroom-like scenes display courtroom-like behavior.

16. Or at least the dollar-book version of Lacan.

17. I base this generalization on fairly extensive discussions about the film with a number of friends, students, and strangers (at a public screening/discussion session), and I refer the reader to the film itself.

18. The Dutch title of this film is *De stilte rond Christina M.*, or, literally translated into the title originally used in English, *The Silence Surrounding Christina M.* It is interesting to wonder what effect this titular duality has had, and still has, on perception of the film. As Ella Shohat and Robert Stam point out, "the title, as that sequence of signs which circulates in the world in the form of advertisement or announcement prior even to the film's screening, constitutes an especially privileged locus in the discursive chain of film" ("The Cinema after Babel: Language, Difference, Power," *Screen* 26.3–4 [1985]: 35–58). Contemplation of the film's original title poses a challenge, I believe, to those who were initially and more copiously exposed to the second translation— namely, the challenge of understanding the film as asymmetrically centered around Christina. Yet it is a challenge that becomes easier to meet with each viewing.

19. See, in this connection, E. Ann Kaplan's discussion of Duras's *Nathalie Granger* in *Women and Film: Both Sides of the Camera* (New York: Methuen, 1983), 91–103.

Filmography

All about Eve (Joseph L. Mankiewicz, United States, 1950)

The American Friend (Wim Wenders, West Germany, 1977)

Anatomy of a Murder (Otto Preminger, United States, 1959)

Bananas (Woody Allen, United States, 1971)

The Birds (Alfred Hitchcock, United States, 1963)

Blow Out (Brian De Palma, United States, 1981)

Blue Velvet (David Lynch, United States, 1986)

Breaker Morant (Bruce Beresford, Australia, 1980)

Casablanca (Michael Curtiz, United States, 1942)

Chinatown (Roman Polanski, United States, 1974)

Citizen Kane (Orson Welles, United States, 1941)

Day for Night (François Truffaut, France/Italy, 1973)

Disbarred (Robert Florey, United States, 1938)

Dream a Little Dream (Marc Rocco, United States, 1989)

8½ (Federico Fellini, Italy, 1963)

A Few Good Men (Rob Reiner, United States, 1992)

Flashdance (Adrian Lyne, United States, 1983)

For Keeps (John G. Avildsen, United States, 1988)

Frankenstein (James Whale, United States, 1931)

Fury (Fritz Lang, United States, 1936)

Gentlemen Prefer Blondes (Howard Hawks, United States, 1953)

I Am a Fugitive from a Chain Gang (Mervyn Le Roy, United States, 1932)

I Confess (Alfred Hitchcock, United States, 1953)

In a Lonely Place (Nicholas Ray, United States, 1950)

In the Name of the Father (Jim Sheridan, Great Britain/Ireland, 1993)

Inherit the Wind (Stanley Kramer, United States, 1960)

It's a Wonderful Life (Frank Capra, United States, 1946)

JFK (Oliver Stone, United States, 1991)

Judgment at Nuremberg (Stanley Kramer, United States, 1961)

The Juror (Brian Gibson, United States, 1996)

Kind Hearts and Coronets (Robert Hamer, Great Britain, 1949)

The Last Wave (Peter Weir, Australia, 1977)

Light of Day (Paul Schrader, United States, 1987)

The Little Mermaid (John Musker and Ron Clements, United States, 1989)

The Lonely Villa (D. W. Griffith, United States, 1909)

M (Fritz Lang, Germany, 1931)

The Man Who Wouldn't Talk (Herbert Wilcox, Great Britain, 1957)

Mary Poppins (Robert Stevenson, United States, 1964)

Miller's Crossing (Joel Coen, United States, 1990)

Miracle on 34th Street (George Seaton, United States, 1947)

Modern Times (Charlie Chaplin, United States, 1936)

Mr. Smith Goes to Washington (Frank Capra, United States, 1939)

Nathalie Granger (Marguerite Duras, France, 1972)

Notorious (Alfred Hitchcock, United States, 1946)

Los Olvidados (Luis Buñuel, Mexico, 1951)

The Ox-Bow Incident (William Wellman, United States, 1943)

Portia on Trial (George Nicholls Jr., United States, 1937)

A Question of Silence (Marleen Gorris, Netherlands, 1982)

Raiders of the Lost Ark (Stephen Spielberg, United States, 1981)

Rashomon (Akira Kurosawa, Japan, 1951)

Rear Window (Alfred Hitchcock, United States, 1954)

La Ronde (Max Ophuls, France, 1950)

The Shining (Stanley Kubrick, Great Britain, 1980)

Silkwood (Mike Nichols, United States, 1983)

Singin' in the Rain (Gene Kelly and Stanley Donen, United States, 1952)

Sirocco (Curtis Bernhardt, United States, 1951)

The Sound of Music (Robert Wise, United States, 1965)

Stage Fright (Alfred Hitchcock, Great Britain, 1950)

Sullivan's Travels (Preston Sturges, United States, 1941)

Sunset Boulevard (Billy Wilder, United States, 1950)

Teenage Mutant Ninja Turtles (Steve Barron, United States, 1990)

Terms of Endearment (James L. Brooks, United States, 1983)

The Thin Blue Line (Errol Morris, United States, 1988)

To Kill a Mockingbird (Robert Mulligan, United States, 1962)

Touch of Evil (Orson Welles, United States, 1958)

Twelve Angry Men (Sidney Lumet, United States, 1957)

Uncle Josh at the Moving Picture Show (Edwin S. Porter, United States, 1902)

Veronika Voss (Rainer Werner Fassbinder, West Germany, 1982)

Vertigo (Alfred Hitchcock, United States, 1958)

What's Up, Doc? (Peter Bogdanovich, United States, 1972)

Witness for the Prosecution (Billy Wilder, United States, 1957)

The Wrong Man (Alfred Hitchcock, 1957)

Yentl (Barbra Streisand, Great Britain, 1983)

Zelig (Woody Allen, United States, 1983)

Index

All about Eve (1953), 18
Allen, Robert C., 45
Allen, Woody, 79–80
Altman, Rick, 62–65, 67–68, 70, 87
American Film Musical, The (Altman), 62–65
American Friend, The (1977), 135
Anatomy of a Murder (1959), 59
Asahina, Robert, 143
Asimow, Michael, 61

Baldwin, Faith, 118
Ball, Lucille, 82
Bananas (1971), 62, 79–80
Barth, John, 50n3
Barthes, Roland, 113
Bazin, André, 130
Bennett, W. Lance, 35, 46–47, 102, 142, 162
Benson, Sheila, 143, 148, 151–53
Bergman, Paul, 61
Bernard, Jami, 143
Bierce, Ambrose, 17
Birds, The (1963), 179
Bleak House (Dickens), 131
Blow Out (1981), 151–53
Blue Velvet (1986), 148
Bogart, Humphrey, 89
Bordwell, David, 28, 104–5, 130; opposed to language-centered film theory, 20–26, 105–6
Breaker Morant (1980), 59

camera: as witness, 103
Camilleri, Marijane, 113–17, 121, 125, 136
Capra, Frank, 129
Casablanca (1942), 121–23, 134
Chanko, Kenneth M., 148
Chatman, Seymour, 15–20, 26
Chinatown (1974), 134
Citizen Kane (1941), 33n31
City of Mobile v. Bolden, 119–21
Cohen-Séat, Gilbert, 33n30
Coleman, John, 143, 148
Committee for the First Amendment, 95n9
Constructivism, 20–21, 23–24, 28, 104–5, 151
corrective criticism, 145; defined, 144
courtroom: as theater, 2
courtroom film, 2, 58, 73–80, 82, 171, 174–77, 179; as genre, 59–61, 64–68
"Court TV," 7
Cover, Robert, 163–68

Day for Night (1973), 57, 69
Denvir, John, 129, 134
De Palma, Brian, 151
Derrida, Jacques, 113
detective, 103; as metaphor for film viewer, 103–6
Dickens, Charles, 45, 131
Disbarred (1938), 118
"Divorce Court," 7

Dream a Little Dream (1989), 157n9
Dunlop, C. R. B., 110–13, 130–31
duration: of on-screen events as criterion for genre membership, 60–61, 66

Ebert, Roger, 44
Edison, Thomas, 56
8½ (1963), 57
Eyewitness Testimony (Loftus), 100

fabula, 24–26; and syuzhet, 25
Fassbinder, Rainer Werner, 57
Feldman, Martha S., 35, 46–47, 102, 142, 162
Fell, John L., 45
Fellini, Federico, 57
Few Good Men, A (1992), 59
film: delimited, 4–5; as narrative regime, 1–2, 34, 39–48; and pleasure, 39–42
film noir, 89
film pedagogy and curriculum, 131–38
Flashdance (1983), 122–23, 126
forensic criticism, 141–42, 145; as argumentation, 145–47; defined, 144; and ethics, 149–52; and politics, 154–56; as rhetoric, 147–49
For Keeps (1988), 148
Foucault, Michel, 113
Frankenstein (1931), 57
Fury (1936), 72, 74, 76–77, 80

Genette, Gérard, 15
genre, 4–5, 58–60
genre theory, 62–65, 70, 87–88
Gentlemen Prefer Blondes (1953), 78–80
Glaspell, Susan, 114–15
Gorris, Marleen, 167
Gospel of St. Mark, 14
Graham, Gloria, 89
Griffith, D. W., 45, 144

Harvey, Stephen, 148
Heinzelman, Susan Sage, 124–25
Helmholtz, Herman Ludwig von, 22
history: and genre, 87–88; and reflexivity, 91–92
Hitchcock, Alfred, 19, 39, 56
Holmes, Oliver Wendell, 129
Hoover, J. Edgar, 80

House Un-American Activities Committee (HUAC), 91–93
Hughes, Dorothy B., 90
hypothesis-testing, 28, 104; in cognition of film, 23–24

I Am a Fugitive from a Chain Gang (1932), 169, 175
I Confess (1953), 169–70
"I Love Lucy," 82
In a Lonely Place (1950), 88–94
Inherit the Wind (1960), 59
In re: Sitkin Smelting and Refining, 123
In the Name of the Father (1993), 183n9
It's a Wonderful Life (1946), 134

Jett, Joan, 122
JFK (1991), 143
Judgment at Nuremberg (1961), 74, 174
Juror, The (1996), 59

Kaplan, E. Ann, 184n19
Kind Hearts and Coronets (1949), 183n9
Kozinski, Alex, 61
Kramer, Stanley, 74

Lang, Fritz, 72, 74, 76
language: denial of, by logocentric regimes, 48–50; in film theory, 22–23; and perception, 21–23. *See also* narrative
Lanham, Richard A., 157n11
Last Wave, The (1977), 9, 167, 178–83
Laurence, Robert, 122–23, 126
law: delimited, 4–5; as narrative regime, 1–2, 34–38, 46–48; and power, 36–39. *See also* law in film; legal procedure
law-and-literature movement, 36–37, 50n2, 110–17, 126, 130, 133–34, 163
law in film: significance of, 1–5, 57–58, 60
legal facts, 104
legal pedagogy, 1; and curriculum, 111–13, 124–26, 130–38. *See also* legal scholarship
legal procedure: cultural relativity of, 47; investigation, 59; punishment, 161–67; trial, 58, 66, 75–76, 100–102. *See also* courtroom; verdict

Legal Reelism: Hollywood Films as Legal Texts (special issue of *Legal Studies Forum*), 129–30
legal scholarship: addressing film, 109–10, 117–19, 121–35; interdisciplinary ("law-and-. . ."), 110–12, 163. *See also* law-and-literature movement; legal pedagogy: and curriculum
Legal Studies Forum, 129–30
Lexis/Nexis, 109
Light of Day (1987), 122–23, 126
Little Mermaid, The (1989), 41
Loftus, Elizabeth, 100, 102–3
Logic of Perception, The (Rock), 21–22
logomorphism, 28–31, 33n30, 38, 42–44, 75–77, 79–80, 99, 101, 103, 107n4, 168, 178–82
Lolita (Nabokov), 20
Lonely Villa, The (1909), 144
Lucia, Cynthia, 9n1
Lumière brothers, 45

M (1931), 59, 66
MacCabe, Colin, 22
Man Who Wouldn't Talk, The (1957), 76, 80
Marshall, Thurgood, 120
Mary Poppins (1964), 41
Messenger, John C., Jr., 47
metaphor: "camera as witness," 99; "witness as camera," 99–103
Metz, Christian, 22, 31, 43, 130
Meyer, Philip N., 126–28, 130
Miller's Crossing (1990), 148
Miracle on 34th Street (1947), 78
Modern Times (1936), 80
Monroe, Marilyn, 78
Morin, Edgar, 31
Mr. Smith Goes to Washington (1939), 129
musicals, 83n6

Nabokov, Vladimir, 20
Narration in the Fiction Film (Bordwell), 20–26
narrative: central to law and film, 13; as choice in film, 43–50; as choice in law, 48–50; distinct from "a narrative," 14; linear and nonlinear, 161; metaphysical behavior of, 15–17, 25–28; verbal,

in relation to visual, 17–24, 169–77; verbal underpinnings of, 14, 20, 24–30, 78, 131–32; working definition of, 31
narrative devices, 16–19, 33n31; description, 16–17; duration, 16; flashback, 17–18, 66, 174–75; pause, 16–17; stretch, 16–17
Nathalie Granger (1972), 184n19
Notorious (1946), 67
nouveau roman, 17

Olvidados, Los (1951), 17
Ox-Bow Incident, The (1943), 59, 66–67

Papke, David, 129
Patrick, Gail, 118
"Perry Mason," 6
phenomenography, 101–3, 107n4
plausibility, 73, 141–42, 144; as criterion of assessment of film, 141–42, 144–45; as criterion of judgment in law, 141–42, 144
Polan, Dana, 88–89
Porter, Edwin S., 56
Portia on Trial (1937), 118
prison, 162; in film, 162, 164–66
probabilism. *See* plausibility
Psychology of Eyewitness Testimony, The (Yarmey), 103

Question of Silence, A (1982), 2, 6, 9, 167–68, 171–78, 182

Raiders of the Lost Ark (1981), 143
Rashomon (1951), 124–26, 134
Ray, Nicholas, 88
realism, 44
Rear Window (1954), 24, 56–57, 105
Reconstructing Reality in the Courtroom (Bennett and Feldman), 35, 102
Reel Justice: The Courtroom Goes to the Movies (Bergman and Asimow), 61–62
reflection (nondisruptive reflexivity), 71–75, 80, 92–94. *See also* reflexivity; refraction (critical reflexivity)
reflexivity, 55–58, 78, 82, 89–90, 183; automatic, 58–61, 65–75, 80, 82, 83n6, 87–88, 92–94; elective, 69–76, 80, 92–94, 164; in grammar, 56

Reflexivity in Film and Literature (Stam), 56

refraction (critical reflexivity), 71–75, 80, 92–94, 164. *See also* reflexivity

rhetoric and rhetorical figures, 148–49

Rock, Irvin, 21–22, 24, 28

Ronde, La (1950), 72

Russell, Jane, 78

Saint Matthew Passion (Bach), 170

Santa Claus, 78

Sarris, Andrew, 143, 149, 156

schemata, 104

Sheffield, Ric, 118–19

Shining, The (1980), 148

Shohat, Ella, 83n24

silence: as antilogomorphic principle, 168–70, 172–77

Silkwood (1983), 143

Singin' in the Rain (1952), 72

Sirocco (1951), 95n8

Siskel, Gene, 43

"Six Million Dollar Man, The," 17

Sklar, Robert, 91

Smith, Barbara Herrnstein, 15–16, 24–26

Soifer, Aviam, 119–23, 126, 134

Sokolow, David Simon, 124–26

Sound of Music, The (1965), 83n6

spectacle: distinct from narrative, 40

Stage Fright (1950), 19

Stam, Robert: on genre, 83n21; on reflexivity, 56–57, 71–72, 74

Stern, Herbert, 166–67

Stewart, Potter, 120

Stone Pillow (made-for-TV movie, 1985), 82

Story and Discourse (Chatman), 15

storytelling. *See* narrative

Strick, Philip, 143

Sullivan's Travels (1941), 169

Sunset Boulevard (1950), 57

"Superior Court," 7

synoptist, 102–3

syuzhet. *See* fabula: and syuzhet

Teenage Mutant Ninja Turtles (1990), 143

television: law represented on, 7

Terms of Endearment (1983), 143

textual determinism, 82, 151

theory: "applying" to new corpus, 83n12

Thin Blue Line, The (1988), 164

Todorov, Tzevetan, 149

To Kill a Mockingbird (1962), 59

Touch of Evil (1958), 94

Travolta, John, 151

trial. *See* legal procedure

Truffaut, François, 57

TV Guide, 15, 39–40

Twain, Mark, 50n3

Twelve Angry Men (1957), 59

Uncle Josh at the Moving Picture Show (1902), 56–57

United States v. Tiede, 166–67

verbal abstraction. *See* narrative

verbal paraphrase. *See* narrative

verbal recountability. *See* narrative

verdict, 39, 75, 78, 104, 161

Veronika Voss (1982), 57, 69

Vertigo (1958), 39, 139n43, 170

Weir, Peter, 167

Welles, Orson, 33n31, 94

West, Robin, 36–37

Westerns, 83n6

What's Up, Doc? (1972), 169

White, Hayden, 113

Wilcox, Herbert, 76

Wilder, Billy, 57

Witness for the Prosecution (1957), 2, 169

Women and Film: Both Sides of the Camera (Kaplan), 184n19

Wrong Man, The (1957), 2

Yarmey, A. Daniel, 103

Yentl (1983), 143, 148

Zelig (1983), 80

David A. Black is an associate professor of communication at Seton Hall University. His work has appeared in *Cinema Journal, Wide Angle,* and *Yale Journal of Criticism.*

Typeset in 10/13 Trump Mediaeval
with Helvetica Neue Black display
Designed by Dennis Roberts
Composed by Jim Proefrock
at the University of Illinois Press
Manufactured by Cushing-Malloy, Inc.